Where Do I Belong?

Where Do I Belong?

A Kids' Guide to Stepfamilies

BUFF BRADLEY

illustrations by Maryann Cocca

Addison-Wesley

Text Copyright © 1982 by Buff Bradley
Illustrations Copyright © 1982 by Maryann Cocca
All Rights Reserved
Addison-Wesley Publishing Company, Inc.
Reading, Massachusetts 01867
Printed in the United States of America

ABCDEFGHIJK-DO-898765432

Library of Congress Cataloging in Publication Data

Bradley, Buff.
       Where do I belong?

       Bibliography: p.
       Includes index.
       Summary: Discusses problems children face when a
parent remarries.
       1. Stepchildren—Juvenile literature.   2. Stepparents
—Juvenile literature.   [1. Stepparents.   2. Divorce.
3. Remarriage]   I. Cocca, Maryann, 1958–   ill.
II. Title.
HQ 777.7.B7   646.7′8   81-43626
ISBN 0-201-10177-7   AACR2
ISBN 0-201-10178-5 pbk

For Gyl Bradley

Many thanks to these people who reviewed the manuscript for this book and offered helpful suggestions:
Myrna Klee, M.S.W.
Sonja Margulies, Associate Editor, *Journal of Transpersonal Psychology*
Dr. Emily Visher, President, Stepfamily Association of America

And many thanks to these stepchildren and stepparents who shared their thoughts and feelings with me:

Bryna Battjes	Bruce George
Leane Battjes	Katy Gibson
Amy Bradley	Rich Kueny
Jeff Buck	Sally Kueny
Sky Dunbar	Tova Rasmussen
Michelle Fadelli	Stacy Remer

Contents

CHAPTER ONE

Beginning with Feelings

It can feel a little odd being a stepchild, not being able to live with both of your parents in the same place at the same time. From time to time your life may seem like a bad photograph—a little out of focus, a little blurred—as you move back and forth between two families, or as your emotions hop around from happiness to sadness to

loneliness to anger to longing. It may seem strange seeing another man—your stepfather—standing where your father once was, or your stepmother standing where your mother was. And maybe you find yourself daydreaming more than you used to—about the parent who is gone, about the way things used to be, about having your family all together again.

Even if the divorce is long past, you still remember it vividly. You may still feel what you felt then and bring those memories and feelings with you into the new family, the stepfamily. You may still be hurt and confused about the divorce, or sad or depressed or even angry that your family broke up. You still want your parents to be together.

Not all stepchildren have all these feelings. Some kids whose parents fought all the time were relieved when their parents divorced and things began to quiet down (though they didn't always quiet down right away, even with one parent out of the house). And some kids feel perfectly happy and comfortable with new stepparents. But for many kids, stepfamilies are a real problem, and you probably wouldn't be reading this book if you weren't one of those kids.

Kids who have very strong feelings about the divorce and the remarriage of one or both of their parents may have a particularly difficult time adjusting to stepfamily life. It's hard for them to get along with their stepparents or their stepbrothers and stepsisters. They long for the parent who is not there. They don't want to share Mom's attention with her new husband or Dad's attention with his new wife. Or they can't get used to having new brothers and sisters all of a sudden. Or they don't feel that they should have to mind someone who isn't a "real" parent. Or they don't want to like a stepparent because they don't want to be disloyal to the parent who is gone. Or they feel guilty because Dad wants them to love his new wife or Mom wants them to love her new husband, and they don't. Emotions and memories swirl around inside them, making a calm and happy stepfamily life seem impossible.

Understanding and Expressing Feelings

This book is mostly about feelings—the feelings you had when your parents divorced and the feelings you have now as a member of a stepfamily. Emotions, even the difficult ones, are a natural part of a full and healthy life. Feelings of anger and joy, excitement and sadness come and go just the way physical hunger and thirst and tiredness come and go. When you're hungry, you eat. When you're tired, you rest. What do you do when you're angry? When you're sad?

Feelings are an important part of your relationships with others, too—the most important part. In order to get along well with the other people in your life, you must freely express what you're feeling. That isn't always easy. Lots of people are shy about expressing their feelings. It may be difficult even to say "I really like you" to a good friend. For some people it's even harder to say "I'm mad at you" or "I'm jealous." And sometimes, even if you'd like to express your feelings, you're confused about what they are.

When you read what feelings many kids have about divorce and stepfamilies, you may recognize some of your own emotions. Because there are so many divorces today, much of *Where Do I Belong?* is about the feelings kids have concerning divorce and how those feelings affect stepfamily life. If you are a stepchild because of the death of one of your parents, those parts of the book about divorce and splitting your time between two families aren't for you. But other problems are the same for stepfamilies that exist because of divorce or because of death, and you will read about these problems in this book, too. It's good to know that you aren't alone, that plenty of others feel what you do. And when you read that there are many ways to express your feelings and to talk with family members about the problems you're having, you will begin to understand that you don't have to keep your emotions locked up inside, making you miserable. You can set them loose. When they're locked up in the dark inside you, emotions are usually more damaging than when they're free and out in the open.

Reading This Book

Chapter two and chapter three of this book are about living through divorce and getting used to life in single-parent households. In one way that's all a part of your past. But in another way it's still a part of your life now. After all, you wouldn't have a stepparent if there hadn't been a divorce. And you may still have many unhappy feelings about that divorce. It takes a long time to get over divorce and it usually takes kids longer than it takes adults. If those feelings are still going on, you must figure them out and then figure out what to do about them.

Chapters four and five are about stepfamilies—what they are and what problems many of them have. Reading that other kids and other stepfamilies have the same problems you do can help you understand that everything in your stepfamily household may not be as unusual and awful as you thought.

The sixth chapter is about what stepparents feel. It always helps people to get along better when each can understand what the other thinks and feels. It may surprise you to learn that your stepparent may be feeling many of the same things you are.

Chapter seven suggests things you can do yourself about what is bothering you. (Other parts of the book also have advice about dealing with problems.) When you're a kid, lots of big decisions are made without you, whether you like them or not—decisions that concern you very much. Divorce is one of them. Becoming a stepfamily is another. There are many things that happen to you that you can't do anything about. But when it comes to *your* feelings, *you're* in charge. Only you can decide whether to meet your problems or try to ignore them. Only you can decide whether to hide your feelings or express them. Only you can choose how you will try to heal the wounds of the past and try to live a satisfying life with both your parents and your stepparents.

CHAPTER TWO

Living Through Divorce

Does it seem like a bad dream to you now—your parents' divorce? You wish it was only a bad dream. Then you could wake up and know that it really didn't happen. But it did happen. It happened to you just as much as it happened to your parents. Somebody left—somebody important to you. Somebody left because the two adults

in the house decided somebody would leave. You were probably surprised when you found out. (Some kids know that constant fighting means serious trouble between their parents. But others think the fights are just a normal part of family life.) Your parents may have said things were bad between them, but still everything seemed fine to you. Or, maybe they didn't tell you until right before it happened. And you were so surprised and confused and scared you couldn't think straight, couldn't even say "Wait!" or "Stop!" or "Don't!" before the door closed.

Parents have a hard time telling their kids about divorce. Some put it off until the very last minute. There are many reasons parents wait so long to tell their kids. But no reason is good enough. Kids have a right to know. They can't make the decision or change anybody's mind, but at least they should have the chance to hear about the divorce long enough before it happens to think about it and ask questions about it. Parents may decide that divorce is good for them. Sometimes they say, "It will be better for you, too. It will be better for all of us. Wait and see." But it didn't feel better to you because the door closed and somebody was gone . . . somebody you love . . . one of your parents.

So Many Emotions

Do you remember some of the things you felt and thought about right at first, when you learned about the divorce?

Talk about strong emotions! If you were like most kids who go through divorce, your mind was like a crowded building in which someone yells "Fire!" Somebody said "Divorce!" You panicked. Your mind went wild. Your emotions ran every which way, stumbling over each other. Your thoughts were so loud and furious you could almost hear them shouting out of your brain.

Fear of Being Left Alone

One of the first things many kids feel is a fear of being left alone. That's one fear we all have, almost from the time we're born. We have it at first because we realize we can't take care of ourselves. The adults take care of us. Usually that's Mother and Father. As we grow, they take care of us less and less and we take care of ourselves more and more until we leave home and are on our own. But even when we can do most things by ourselves, it feels good and safe to have them there, making a home for us, watching over things, helping out when something goes wrong. We want them to *be there* for us.

When your parents got divorced, your imagination started working overtime. You thought, "If they stopped loving each other, they can stop loving me and go away." One parent left; you worried that the other parent might decide to leave at any time, and you'd be all alone.

If you weren't afraid that you'd be left alone by both parents, you might still have worried that the parent who was moving out of the house would go away forever. You were afraid that you'd never see that parent again—left alone by one parent if not by two.

It would have helped very much if your parents had talked to you about this fear, if they had sat down with you and said, "Look, we're getting divorced from each other but not from you. We're both still your parents. We're both going to keep taking care of you. You'll live with one of us and visit the other regularly." Or, "You'll live with each of us half the time." "You're very important to both of us and we'll never leave you."

Did your parents say anything like that when they were getting divorced? If they did, it helped you to be a little less afraid, and you're lucky because many, many kids say that their parents didn't take any time to have that kind of talk. Some parents were so busy fighting with each other they seemed to forget the kids were there. Other parents seemed so hurt and depressed that they could barely talk about anything. It wasn't fair that they didn't try to give some reassurance to their frightened children. It just wasn't fair.

Confusion and Guilt

When you were little, about two or three years old, you probably asked "Why?" about everything.

"It's time to eat breakfast."

"Why?"

"Don't hit your brother."

"Why?"

"Put your toys away."

"Why?"

"Why do dogs bark? Why is the sky blue? Why is the grass green? Why is it winter? Why can't I be ten?" And then, later, you asked, "Why? Why are they getting a divorce?"

Divorce is often confusing to the adults who have decided to separate. They may feel unsure of themselves, not knowing what they really want, wondering if a divorce will actually make things better, wondering how well they'll do on their own.

If divorce is confusing to adults, it's a thousand times more confusing to kids. "How can this happen? Did they fall out of love? How can you just stop loving someone? Maybe it's because of the fights. They fight a lot, but they don't fight all the time. They fight about money, and they fight about me. If it weren't for me, they wouldn't fight so much. It's because of me. They're getting divorced because of me. If I weren't so bad they wouldn't be getting divorced."

Because you were confused and didn't know why your parents were getting divorced, you started imagining all sorts of reasons. Eventually almost all kids imagine that the divorce is their fault. Maybe you thought that. Maybe you still think it. It's just not true. Kids don't cause divorces. Two people decide not to live together anymore; nobody *makes* them come to that decision. Two parents could have the absolute worst kids in the world, and if they *wanted* to stay together, they *would*, no matter how horrible the kids were.

Did your parents tell you why they were getting divorced? Many parents say such things as "It's an adult problem, and you wouldn't understand it." But even if you didn't understand it, it would help to hear some kind of explanation. Other parents do try to explain, and it *is* hard to understand.

> "We've made a very difficult decision. We've decided to get a divorce."
> "Why?"
> "We just haven't been getting along for more than a year now."
> "Why?"
> "We've grown apart in so many ways. We're like strangers to each other."
> "Why?"
> "We loved each other once, but we just don't love each other anymore."
> Why? . . . Why?. . . Why? . . . Why? . . . Why?

A Broken Bond

In the eighteenth century in France, criminals were sometimes punished in a very brutal way. Ropes were tied first to each arm and each leg. Then each rope was tied to a different horse, and the horses were driven off in four different directions. It may have felt like that to you when your parents were divorcing—your mother galloping off in one direction, your father galloping off in another direction. You were being pulled both ways at once. It was tearing you apart.

Your connection with your parents is a strong one. They're the people who gave you life and who took care of you when you were too little to take care of yourself. They're the people who taught you to walk and to talk. They're the people who helped you learn about the world—that fire was hot, that running across the street was dangerous, that you didn't have to be afraid of thunder. They woke you up in the morning and put you in bed at night. You spent more time with your parents than with anybody else. You didn't all just happen to be together at the same place, at the same time. You were *joined* together—by love, yes, but also by the support you received from and gave to each other, by all the experiences you shared, by knowing each other better than anybody else knew any of you.

So when your parents split up, you felt that connection split, too. That bond that you felt deep inside you,

that held your family together, was breaking apart. And you felt that you were being torn into pieces.

Parents who realize that their kids feel this way—as if they're being split in half—will try to help them by talking to them and especially by *listening* to them. To talk and be listened to doesn't always make the pain go away, but it can often make the pain less intense. It's always better to express what you're feeling and thinking than it is to hold it all inside. And it's good to know that someone else understands, or at least wants to understand.

There are many parents, of course, who are very troubled by their own divorces. Even when they want to divorce, going through it all can be painful for them, too. They think so much about their own problems that they don't take the time to think about their kids' problems. If the kids aren't acting crazy or sobbing all the time or breaking things or running away, these parents may think that the kids are just fine. They don't know about the ropes, and the horses galloping off in opposite directions.

Helplessness

Canute was a Danish king of England about a thousand years ago. Like all kings, Canute was a powerful man who could order people about. In fact, he figured he was so powerful that he could even get the ocean tides to stop. He stood on the shore and commanded the tides to cease. He shouted and shouted, but the waters roared back and the tides just kept on. There were limits to Canute's power.

There are different kinds of power. One kind is being able to do what you want to do, to accomplish what you want on your own. It is being independent, being responsible. Another kind of power is getting people to do things you want them to do. Kings like Canute might order underlings about. Do this! Do that! But ordinary people have other ways. Some try to persuade people to do things by talking with them and convincing them. You probably know "persuaders" like that. Also, you probably know people who flatter or tease or bully or whine or have tantrums or beg or play helpless or argue to get others to do something.

There's nothing admirable about fooling people or forcing them to do what you want. But doing things on your own is a good kind of power. As you grow up, you are able to do more and more on your own, for yourself. And usually that feels just fine.

Then divorce happens; it hurts and there is nothing you can do about it. You don't feel strong and independent and responsible. You feel helpless, out of control. Like a huge wave, divorce crashes down on you and you cannot command it to stop.

When you feel out of control you don't feel safe. Old King Canute wasn't satisfied just to have power over people. He wanted power over the forces of nature also. He couldn't feel truly safe unless he could command nature to do what he bade. You know how he felt. If divorce happened to you, you thought, then other terrible things could happen, too, other terrible things you couldn't do anything about. If you couldn't make your parents love each other and stay together, then you couldn't make them love you and stay with you.

Of course you can never be absolutely safe. Many things happen over which you have no control. And when they do happen, particularly if they cause you pain, you can feel small, insignificant, and frightened. Part of growing up has to do with being able to accept the fact that you cannot control everything. You have to learn to live with some uncertainty, to absorb the blows of chance and circumstance, and still live your life as fully as you can. But that doesn't mean you have to like everything that happens, and it doesn't mean that you won't feel helpless and unsafe from time to time.

After going through a divorce, many kids feel so helpless that they just stop being responsible. They try to become babies again so that the grown-ups will take care of everything and protect them from harm. (It isn't just kids who do this. Adults do it too.) It's okay to want to be babied once in a while, as long as it doesn't go on too long, but it's very disappointing to want to be babied and not have anybody willing to baby you. Many newly divorced parents are too involved in their own troubles to notice when their kids want and need some extra, special attention.

Other kids don't seem to want to be babied at all. They start doing more and more, working more around the house, working extra hard in school, helping more

with little brothers and sisters. Some kids do all this because they feel they must take care of their parents. They're worried that if they don't take on extra responsibilities their newly divorced parents, who may be feeling very miserable, will just fall apart. It's pretty tough for a kid to be a parent to a parent.

Other kids start doing more because they recognize that, while there are some big things like marriage and divorce that they can't control, there are other things that they can take care of quite well. Kids who feel helpless after a divorce can help themselves by keeping busy doing what they do well—playing the guitar, making models, playing soccer, inventing computer games, writing stories, drawing, even things like cleaning and rearranging their rooms and making their own lunches. Keeping busy will help remind them that they can do many things on their own, that they aren't totally helpless.

Your parents divorced, and you felt helpless and afraid. Because it hurt so much and you were so frightened, you may have decided to protect yourself by never loving anybody else—anybody else who could go away, too. It's natural to want to do that, but it's not such a good idea. What you're really doing is putting yourself in a cage, where nobody can get to you and you can't get to anybody else. It may be safer in your cage, but it's lonely, and you're a prisoner.

Other Fears and Worries

"Ghoulies and ghosties and long-legged beasties, and things that go bump in the night." There are many things people fear. Some of them are real, and some of them are imagined. When your parents divorced, your imagination started producing all sorts of scary possibilities. Besides your fears of being left completely alone and of never seeing one of your parents again, you felt other fears and worries as well.

Money. One thing parents seem to argue a great deal about is money. You may have witnessed many family fights about money. It never seemed that there was enough money, and who spent it and how caused much conflict. Then there was going to be a divorce and two households to support. You were afraid that there wouldn't be enough money to buy food and clothes for you. To make it worse, your parents may have threatened each other by saying such things as: "You're not going to get a penny out of me!" Or a parent who was worried about new money problems may have complained: "I just don't know where the money is going to come from. I don't know how we're going to make it." And you had visions of wearing raggedy clothes and going hungry.

Some parents realize their kids worry about money when the divorce is happening and take the time to reassure them that no matter what the angry words suggest, they're not going to go hungry. Divorce often does mean less money for both new households, and things can be more difficult for some time. That may mean a change in life-style—not so many new clothes and toys, more hamburger and less steak. But families adjust to these changes, and the kids don't have to take to the streets to beg.

Even though the financial responsibility for the family is the parents', not the children's, it's hard not to worry when you see your parents worry. Parents should understand this and talk to their kids about money. But as you've seen, parents don't always realize what their kids are feeling. If your parents didn't talk to you about money, you may have suffered money worries as much as they did.

Moving. When your family world is falling apart, it's easy to think that the rest of your world will fall apart, too. Outside the family your world includes neighborhood, school, friends. If you are worried about money, you also worry that you'll have to move to a smaller house or apartment. That might mean leaving your school, your neighborhood, and your friends. At a time in your life when you are feeling your worst, you need some things that are stable and familiar. It's hard enough to move to a new place, go to a new school, try to make new friends when things are terrific at home. To move away when things are terrible seems too much to bear.

And maybe your worry came true. Many families do move after divorce. Some parents move their families right away because they can't afford to stay where they are. Others move to get a "fresh start," without realizing that the last thing in the world their kids want is a fresh start.

Being "weird."   Today there are a million divorces every year in the United States, involving two million adults and more than a million children. You may know a number of kids whose parents are divorced. Yet even though divorce is common, many kids think that being a member of a divorced family makes them unusual. They feel that they aren't normal, that they are "weird" or "strange." Because of this feeling, they often don't tell anybody about the divorce—not their friends, not their teachers, not anybody.

With all the divorces occurring, why should you have felt weird? Maybe it was because you had some strong idea about what a "normal" family is. People often think that a normal family is what is called the nuclear family—a mother, a father, and one or more children, all living together. That was the kind of family you were used to—before the divorce. It was the kind of family you grew up in, the kind of family you knew well. It was the kind of family most of your friends were in. So it always seemed right, normal, perfectly natural to you, so natural that you didn't even think about it. It was also the kind of family you saw all the time on television, in commercials as well as the shows: mother, father, kids—one big, happy family. No wonder it felt strange no longer to be part of that kind of family. No wonder you felt as if you were some kind of freak. (As you'll see in chapter four, the nuclear family isn't the only normal family. The fact is, there are all kinds of families, and the nuclear family is only one of them.)

Embarrassment. You may have felt ashamed that your parents divorced. It can be embarrassing when two adults can't solve their problems in any other way than by splitting up. It can also be embarrassing when you tell people about the divorce and they ask all sorts of questions about it. They want to know why, and *you* can't even figure out why. You don't want to talk about the problems, the arguments, the anger, the pain.

When you experienced the pain of divorce, you might have felt wounded, and that made you especially shy and self-conscious. It made you feel as if there were something wrong with you. You were missing a parent all of a sudden, and it felt almost as if you were no longer a whole person. Maybe you thought that people would treat you differently. Maybe you thought that your friends would no longer be your friends.

After a while, of course, everybody knows about the divorce. It could be a good thing that people finally know. Your teachers may become more understanding, if you've been having trouble in school. Your friends may help with sympathy and concern. You might find that you can talk to some of them about what you are feeling.

When you're feeling terrible and there's nothing you can do to change the situation, talking with a sympathetic friend can help. When you're hungry, you should eat. When you're tired, you should sleep. When you have strong feelings, you should express them; you shouldn't keep them bottled up inside.

Anger and Hurt

When the Queen guessed Rumpelstiltskin's real name, the old dwarf got so mad he stomped himself right into the ground. Can you understand being that angry? Perhaps when your parents divorced you were angry at them, after the shock wore off a little and you had time to think about it. "How can they *do* this to me?" *Stomp-stomp.* "Can't they see how much it hurts me?" *Stomp-stomp.* "They don't care about me! All they care about is themselves!" *Stomp-stomp.* "They're mean and selfish!" *Stomp-stomp.* "I hate them both! I hate them!" *Stomp-stomp.*

Much anger comes from hurt. If you wanted to speak kindly of old Rumpelstiltskin, you could say that the reason he got so angry wasn't because the Queen beat him at his own game. It could have been because he couldn't keep the baby that he really wanted, and that hurt him very much.

Whether you are right about Rumpelstiltskin or not, it's a safe guess that your anger toward your parents at the time of their divorce came from hurt. It hurt you terribly that your family was breaking apart. It hurt to think about one of your parents being gone, and maybe they didn't seem to understand how much you were hurting. Maybe they didn't seem to care, and that made you madder still. You got into fights with them and you were still mad, and you got into fights with brothers and sisters and got into fights with friends. It seemed that you were mad all the time, at everybody.

You may have felt that your parents were just going on their merry ways, tearing up the family, and ignoring what you felt about the whole thing. By getting angry at them you showed how strong your feelings were. And, of course, you hoped that if they finally realized how you were feeling, they'd reconsider and call the whole thing off.

Another thing about anger is that it keeps your mind off the pain. You keep yourself so busy stomping around and shouting and fighting with everybody, making so much noise, that you don't hear that sad little voice inside you saying, "Ouch. It hurts so much. Please make it stop."

After you've been terribly angry and had a bad fight with someone, you might feel ashamed and guilty. Maybe you think you were acting like a two-year-old having a tantrum. Maybe you used a lot of unkind, hurting words, and you wish you hadn't. You didn't really mean them.

You might feel so bad that you vow you'll never let yourself get angry again.

Anger is a tricky emotion to deal with. It's not good to try to hold it inside because it can either build and build until it explodes, or it can make you sick. On the other hand, it's not such a good idea to turn anger into an attack and say all sorts of cruel things that can create problems. What's the solution? It's hard to say. Maybe you beat up your pillow with a tennis racket. Maybe you run ten miles or punch a punching bag or chop wood or break an old toy into smithereens or hike out into the forest and holler at the top of your lungs. Maybe you keep hollering at someone else, but instead of hollering "You're stupid and mean and I hate you!" you holler "I'm mad! Don't do this! It hurts!"

Numbness and Sadness

People often get emotionally numb when something bad happens to them. If that happened to you after your parents' divorce, you felt completely drained of energy. You felt lifeless. Numbness replaced most of your emotions—the ones you liked feeling as well as the ones you didn't like. You had a hard time getting out of bed in the morning. You sat and stared at the television or a wall for hours at a time. You stopped playing with friends, didn't do your schoolwork, and found it difficult to carry on even a simple conversation. You didn't care whether you went to the movies or not, ate dinner or not, visited grandparents or not. Everything seemed too difficult and tiring. Nothing seemed to matter.

Numbness usually happens when a feeling or an emotion is too painful. You couldn't stand to feel the hurt of divorce anymore, so numbness came and shut out the hurt. But in order to do that, numbness had to shut out all emotions. So not only didn't you feel the hurt, you also didn't feel happy, didn't feel excited, didn't feel playful or enthusiastic. The fact is, you didn't feel much of anything except very, very tired.

Whether you grow numb or not when your parents are divorced, you surely are sad. When you lose something or someone dear to you, it's natural to feel sad. If you try not to feel sad, you are trying to pretend that nothing has happened. The longer you pretend, the longer it is before the wounds of divorce begin to heal.

Numbness may give you an emotional rest you need for a while. And sadness is natural and necessary. But if either of them goes on too long, it's unhealthy. Anyone who stays terribly sad for a long, long time, or who grows numb to emotions over and over and over again, should probably see a counselor. A counselor is someone who has had special training to help others deal with their problems. A counselor can be a doctor, a minister, a psychologist, or a social worker associated with your school or church or a Mental Health Center.

Sometimes it can be easier to talk with counselors than with anybody else. A counselor's job is to listen to you. A counselor isn't interested in taking sides or telling you that what you're feeling is mistaken. It feels good to talk and have someone really listen. Too often people don't listen carefully to what others say. Instead, they may be listening to their own thoughts or getting an answer ready while somebody else is talking. When someone really listens to you, that person can really understand. A good counselor can understand even your most confused feelings and maybe help you understand them better, too. A good counselor can help you deal with your hurt feelings and help keep you from becoming so numb and depressed that you feel more dead than alive most of the time.

When you're feeling the pain of your parents' divorce, when one of your parents has left and your whole life has broken apart, it's hard to imagine you'll ever feel good again. But it *is* possible to be happy again. It is possible to have loving relationships with each of your parents, even though you're not all living together anymore. It will take time, and you will spend much of that time feeling sad. Remember, though, that sadness is not only the emotion of endings. It is also the necessary preparation for new beginnings.

CHAPTER THREE

After the Divorce

In dreams sometimes we see ourselves as houses. Divorce was not a welcome guest in your life's house. It didn't knock politely and ask to come in. It broke down the door and crashed through the rooms like a wild bull.

Your life is not a house you can leave. You have to live in the wreckage. Harder even than dealing with the first shock of divorce for many kids is learning to live in the post-divorce family.

Custody

Once your parents decided to divorce, many other decisions became necessary. The next big decision was about custody—which parent you were going to live with. Once again, it was a decision made by parents. At first, that may have seemed unfair to you. But think about it. Wouldn't it have been hard for you to choose between your parents? It might have seemed that you were being asked to pick a favorite parent, or you might have felt that choosing to live with one parent would have been taking sides. It's hard for kids to take sides in a divorce. They want everybody on the *same* side. So really, it's best for parents to make custody decisions.

That doesn't mean that kids shouldn't be asked about what they'd like. When parents and kids can talk together about what everybody needs and wants and what would work the best, kids feel better about it. When parents just announce "It's going to be like this," it hurts and often makes kids feel like property, like tables and chairs, instead of people.

But many parents keep fighting with each other right through the divorce and for a long time afterward. That usually means they don't sit down together with their kids to discuss custody. In fact, some of their worst fights may be about custody, and while they shout and storm about, the kids stand by helplessly, wondering, "What's going to happen to me?"

How was custody settled in your family? After divorce most kids live with their mothers and visit with their fathers on weekends, holidays, and vacations. Some kids live with their fathers and visit their mothers. Some families arrange for the kids to spend equal amounts of time with each parent. Sometimes that means half the week with one parent, half with the other; or two weeks here, two weeks there; or a month at a time in each place. This kind of arrangement allows parents equal responsibility in raising the kids. It also gives kids a chance to be truly at home with each parent. If you live with one parent and visit the other, you know it can be very uncomfortable to feel like a guest in one parent's home. You want to feel that you belong in both places, but in one place you feel almost like a stranger.

However your parents worked out custody, you probably weren't too happy with it. What you really wanted was for your whole family to get back together. Living with one parent and visiting the other, or living with each parent half time, isn't such a terrific life.

Custody decisions are often made when tempers are hottest. When your parents are so very angry with each other, it is difficult for you to approach them to talk about custody arrangements. But after a while things will cool down. Then it may become easier to discuss your feelings about custody. If you'd like to visit your father more than once a month, say so. If you'd like to spend only half the summer away at your mother's so you can have the other half at home near your friends, say so. Custody and visiting should be flexible enough to change as your wants and needs change.

Of course, there is no perfect solution to the problem

of custody and visiting. The best that can be expected is having some way to see both parents as much as possible. But that's nothing compared to the dream that most kids dream, of having the family back together again.

The Dream of Reunion

In your family album there is a picture of all of you together—you and your parents, maybe brothers and sisters. You're all happy, smiling. You remember the day the picture was taken—a holiday celebration or a birthday party or a picnic. It was a wonderful day. Nobody fought. Everybody had a good time and loved each other. Everything was perfect.

Divorce came and tore up your family, but it didn't tear up that picture. The picture stayed in the album and it stayed in your mind.

Most divorced kids carry that picture with them for years and years. The picture is a memory, and it's also a wish, a wish that Mom and Dad would get back together and live happily ever after. "If they were happy together once, they could be happy again," you think. "If I can just figure out how to get them together . . . If I can just figure out how to get them to realize that they love each other . . . ."

You hoped that when your parents saw how miserable and angry the divorce made you, they'd change their minds. You thought you could show them just how unhappy you really were by getting into a lot of trouble at school or running away from home. Then they'd have to get together to have conferences with teachers or to hunt for you or wait until the police found you. And once they got together, they'd want to stay together, and . . . .

A family photograph is only the picture of an instant. It can't show the long, difficult hours, days, years, filled with problems. Your dream left out all the unhappy times, all the fights and tears, all the long, angry silences. Your parents got divorced because they couldn't get along. They probably tried for a long time to solve their problems with each other. When they finally decided they couldn't solve those problems, they chose divorce. It isn't very likely that kids can do anything to get their parents to change their minds.

It feels good to look through the pages of the family album and remember happier times. It's like taking a little vacation in the past. But you learn, as most kids of divorce do, that you can't stay in the past forever, and the wish to have things just as they were "once upon a time" almost never comes true.

New Relationships with Your Parents

Divorce changed your relationship with each of your parents. Some of the changes may have been for the worse. Other changes may actually have been for the better. It may have been the first time you saw your parents as individual people instead of as a unit—*Parent.* It may also have been the first time you had a chance to see your parents' feelings fully exposed.

Living with Your Parents' Feelings

The divorce isn't over when the family splits up. Often both adults have very strong feelings that last for a long time after the divorce is final. If either or both of your parents had a hard time after the divorce, that made it hard for you, too.

Just as you were depressed and angry, your parents may have been depressed and angry. Even though both parents sign the divorce papers, one of them may not have wanted the divorce. That parent in particular is likely to feel terrible. Even when both parents agree that they want to divorce, they may be very unhappy because they think they've failed. They may be unhappy not to come home to a full house anymore. They may feel afraid for the future. In other words, they may have the same feelings their kids do.

Depression.   It was hard enough for you to live with your own sadness and depression. Living with a parent's depression was even harder. You needed a lot of attention, a lot of affection, opportunities to talk about how you were feeling. Your depressed parent didn't have the energy to give you what you needed. Maybe he or she spent most of the time in bed. Many depressed people sleep as much as they can. Maybe there was a lot of drinking, a lot of crying and saying such things as "I don't know what we're going to do." It was very frightening for you to see your parent like that. You counted on that parent for support. You counted on that parent to keep things running smoothly, but that parent didn't seem able to do much of anything. Once again, you felt helpless. Once again, you wondered, "What's going to happen to me?"

Anger.   As we've seen, there's often much anger during and after a divorce—yours and your parents'. One angry parent may have said terrible things about the other and tried to get you to take sides against the other. Many divorced kids say that this angry name-calling is one of the hardest things for them to take. They love *both* their parents and don't want to take sides. They love *both* their parents and don't want to hear one say bad things about the other.

Sometimes it isn't so easy to keep from taking sides when you see that one parent has been particularly hurt by the divorce. That can make you angry enough to blame the other parent—especially since the divorce has hurt you, too. Also, if one parent tries to get you to take sides, you might think you're being disloyal to him or her if you *don't* do it. It can be a real problem.

Some kids try to ignore their parents' anger at each other. They pretend they don't hear the nasty words. They refuse to take sides. Some of them are able to talk to their parents about it: "Look, I know you're angry, but he's my dad and it makes me very unhappy to hear all this bad stuff about him all the time."

Jealousy.   One reason for anger is jealousy. Sometimes when one divorced parent becomes involved with a new person, the other parent gets jealous and angry. Sometimes that new person was involved *before* the divorce and is blamed for causing the divorce. This anger may be intense and it may affect the kids: "I'm not letting you visit your father if *that woman* is going to be there." The parent who makes such threats and who keeps kids from seeing an absent parent is being spiteful and trying to punish his or her former mate. It's pretty childish behavior.

Kids may not be too enthusiastic about the new person in Mom's or Dad's life (see Parents Dating, page 47), but they don't want to let one parent's jealously and anger interfere in the relationship with the other parent. Once again, kids can feel disloyal to the jealous parent by wanting to see their other parent even though there's a new person involved. But most important to kids are the continuing relationships with each parent, and a parent's jealousy and anger shouldn't interfere with that. Kids can help themselves best in this kind of situation by explaining their feelings: "I'm not going to see her; I'm going to see my dad. Please don't stop me from seeing Dad just because you're mad about her. That hurts me just as much as it hurts Dad."

Dependence. Parents are often more lonely than angry after a divorce. There's an empty space in life where a person used to be. Some parents will try to get you to fill that empty space. Sometimes parents start depending on their kids emotionally. It's almost as if the parents become kids themselves. But kids are supposed to depend on parents, not the other way around. If a parent starts depending on you for emotional support, as if you were another adult, it is a heavy burden for you. At first it may feel good. You may feel like a real grown-up. But after a while you begin to feel that you aren't always strong enough to listen to your parent's problems and always be cheerful and always be comforting. It gets very hard, and you wish you were just a kid again.

Of course it may be that your parents didn't have many emotional problems after the divorce, or if they were badly depressed or angry or too dependent on you, perhaps those feelings didn't last long. Still, there were plenty of problems in just getting used to the new life you had with each parent.

The Parent You Live With

Before the divorce you may have been used to having a parent around most of the time. If your father worked away from home, maybe your mother stayed home, or vice versa. If they both worked away from home, maybe they arranged it so that one of them would send you off to school and be there when you got home. The divorce changed all that. There were no longer two parents at home to share the responsibilities of earning a living, taking care of the house, and being with you. Perhaps your mother started working away from the house full-time. All of a sudden there was a big rush in the morning to get everybody out the door so Mom could get to work on time. When you came home from school, you had to let yourself in—to an empty house. You felt lonely in the house by yourself. There was nobody to talk to, nobody to tell about your day. At the end of the day your mother came home so tired from working that she didn't have the energy to prepare the wonderful meals your family used to have. Then, in the evening, instead of sitting down and talking or working together on homework or playing a game, everybody had to rush around and do the household chores that didn't get done during the day. Then it was time for bed. You might have felt that you'd lost *both* parents. One parent moved out. The other one was so busy there wasn't any time for the two of you to be together. This happened when you were feeling so bad about the divorce and especially needed the comfort a parent could give.

Did you ever talk to your parent about it? Did you ever say "I'm lonely. Please spend some time with me."? For some reason, just saying a few simple words such as those can seem like the hardest thing in the world to do. It isn't always easy for kids to tell their parents what they're feeling. Yet there's nothing more important in families, including divorced families, than people talking with each other—not talking about TV and the weather but talking about what they're feeling. Feelings are important. They can keep people apart or bring them together.

New responsibilities. Some of the changes that took place after your parents' divorce may have had their good points as well as their bad. In the single-parent household you had to do more chores than you were used to. It's hard to imagine any kid welcoming more chores, but as much as you disliked the extra work, it just might have made you feel more grown-up, more like a working partner in the household, with important responsibilities.

New happiness. Flowers bloom—and people bloom, too. Once some of the unhappiness of the divorce passed, you may have seen your parent become more relaxed, more cheerful. Just like divorced kids, many divorced parents wonder how they're going to manage after the family splits up. When they begin to discover they *can* manage, they begin to enjoy new feelings of independence and self-confidence. You can see those feelings in the way they look and the way they act. Maybe your parent bought some new clothes, got a new hair-

style, laughed much more than he or she had in a long
time. Sometimes this kind of change for the better can be
hard for kids to accept. Kids get used to their parents
being certain kinds of people, behaving in certain ways.
Divorced kids can get used to a parent's misery, and when
the misery goes away, kids might feel that the parent is
going away or becoming a brand new, completely unfa-
miliar person. And they don't like it. Maybe you felt like
that when your parent started to perk up. On the other
hand, even if you weren't over your own unhappiness, it
may have given you a lift to see your parent in such good
spirits. Maybe things began to seem much more steady
when your parent was happy, confident, and positive.

Closeness.   Did it ever seem to you not only that
adults were older and bigger than kids, but also that they
were different beings? Did your parents ever seem myste-
rious and faraway? Did you wonder what they thought
about and how they felt? Did they seem to be closer to
each other than they were to you? Did you sometimes
think that you'd never really know them?

Living with one parent after the divorce could change
all that. Without another adult around all the time, single
parents often spend much more time talking with their
kids. It is a brand-new relationship for both of you.
Before, it may often have seemed as if the adults were on
one side, the kids on the other side. But after the divorce,
you get to know your parent better. You share some of
the same problems adjusting to the divorce. You see more
clearly that he or she has the same kinds of feeling you

have. You discuss things with each other. You begin to feel that you and your parent are on the *same* side.

The Parent You Don't Live With

Did it ever seem to you as if the parent who moved out became a ghost? Even though he was gone, his spirit stayed in the house. There were reminders of him every-where—a favorite chair, a toy of yours he fixed, pictures in the family album. As each memory appeared, you tried to hold onto it. It was almost as if by remembering every possible detail about him you could magically turn all those memories into a real person—your parent. And there he'd be, home again.

But you can't build a person from memories. Even the strongest memories are ghostly; when you try to hang on tight, they slip out of your grasp.

Maybe the hardest thing of all after the divorce was the new relationship between you and the parent you no longer lived with.

Visits.   In Greek mythology there is a creature called a centaur. It is half man and half horse. That parent who left your everyday life—for most kids it's the father— became a new kind of creature: half parent and half stranger. It was very hard to figure out how to be with him. When you were all living together, he was just there. You probably never thought much about what to say to him, about how to act, about how to pass the time together.

But with that new half parent/half stranger it was all different. You wondered if he still loved you. On your visits you felt shy. You didn't know what to talk about, or

you talked too much because you didn't want him to think you were bored. You tried very hard to be interested and interesting—funny, helpful, enthusiastic about every-thing—so that he'd want you to come again. That's what really made you nervous, even if you didn't admit it to yourself. Somehow you had the feeling that if you weren't the "perfect guest," he might not want you to visit again.

And those visits were precious. If you ever had any negative thoughts about that parent before the divorce, after the divorce you probably forgot them all. You remembered him as almost perfect, and your loneliness for him was very, very strong. Each visit was a reunion that was very happy and very sad at the same time—happy because of your joy at being together again, sad because you couldn't be together all the time.

On the day of a visit maybe you'd get ready hours early and sit out on the front steps, waiting. If he was late, you felt terrible. If he called and said he couldn't make it for some reason, you tried to be understanding, but it hurt so much you could hardly bear it. And if visits were canceled over and over again, instead of feeling all that pain, you probably began to think: "I hate him. I don't ever want to see him again. If he comes to see me, I won't even talk to him." What you were really feeling was: "Why doesn't he love me? There must be something wrong with me."

There are all sorts of reasons why absent parents don't visit their kids. None of them has anything to do with the kids. It's not a child's fault when a parent misses visits and birthdays and doesn't write or call. The parent is the one who is responsible. Sometimes absent parents feel guilty about the divorce and about leaving their children. Every time they see their kids, they feel more guilty. So they stay away because they can't bear the guilt. Other parents feel such pain at living apart from their kids that seeing the kids makes the pain worse. So they stay away. Still other parents want to put the past entirely behind them and not be reminded of it. They think of their kids as part of the past—even though they're really a part of the present—and don't go to see them. These are all understandable reasons, but they aren't excuses. There are no excuses.

Even if your absent parent and you visited regularly from the very beginning and you never had any strong feelings of being abandoned by him, you ran into other problems.

Back and forth. It wasn't easy getting used to your parent's new place. Maybe it was a small apartment with no place that was just for you. When you were there, you felt like a visitor. You didn't feel as if you really belonged. If you were lucky, you did have your own place—a bedroom maybe, or even just a dresser or a closet in which you could keep some of your belongings all the time.

It also wasn't easy getting used to going back and forth between two homes. At one place you had friends in the neighborhood; at the other place you didn't know anybody. At one place you had your bike, your books, your toys, your records; at the other place you had a few things, maybe, and whatever you brought along in your suitcase. At one place you slept in your own room, in your own bed; at the other place you slept on a cot or on a couch or in a sleeping bag on the floor. At one place the refrigerator was filled with certain kinds of food; at the other place it was filled with completely different kinds. At one place you had chores and a bedtime; at the other place you had neither. One place had a color TV; the other place had no TV at all. You began to feel like one of those mythical creatures—half Here-I-Am, half There-I-Am.

Visit or party?   The places you lived were different. The *way* you lived at each place was different, too. In the place where you lived most of the time, life was pretty ordinary. You went to school, did chores, saw your friends. But at your other parent's place, it was all different. Just as you were worried about being a good guest so the visits would continue, your parent was probably worried about being a good host so you'd want to come back. He probably planned all sorts of trips to the movies, the zoo, the planetarium, the beach, and maybe he bought you lots and lots of presents. Every visit was like a birthday party, but as much as you liked movies and presents, you probably began to want things to be more normal. You wanted some ordinariness in the visits. You understood, maybe even without realizing that you knew it, that the real bond between parent and child is formed just by being together in normal ways—hanging around the house, going to the grocery store, washing the car—not by entertaining each other. You wanted your parent to be that kind of parent, a true parent, not a rich uncle.

"Perfect" visits.   Because you didn't get to see your absent parent all the time, you wanted to pack *everything* into your short visits. That's like cramming all your possessions into the overnight bag you carry with you. They won't all fit. But wanting to do that, and wanting to make every visit wonderful and perfect, made you emotional and nervous. (Your parent probably felt the same way.) When you're feeling that way, it's easy for things to go wrong. Sometimes they did go wrong. Sometimes there were misunderstandings. Sometimes there were angry fights. A fight on one of those visits could feel a hundred times worse than a fight at home. At home you had plenty of time to relax and work things out. On visits there was never enough time to let the bad feelings dissolve, to forgive and forget, to come together again before you had to pack up and leave. So instead of being just perfect, things could turn out the opposite, and visits could be disasters. When that happened, you spent the time between visits worrying, promising it wouldn't happen again, and planning the next perfect visit. You got so worked up and tense that the same thing happened the next time. By wanting things to be perfect, you seemed to assure that they wouldn't be.

Most kids eventually learn not to expect perfection. They learn that just like life at home, life on visits can have problems without meaning the end of the world. However strange the visiting situation is, it's still a family situation. Parents and kids are connected by a bond even stronger than husbands and wives. Not a fight on Saturday afternoon, not even a divorce, is likely to break that bond.

Sisters and brothers.   Having sisters and brothers can make visits with a parent more difficult for all of you. With sisters and brothers around, there's never any chance for you and your parent to pay attention only to each other. There's so much to say. You want to talk about everything that's happened in your life since your last visit. You don't want to lose touch. (And, of course, that's the way it is for your sisters and brothers, too.) Maybe you and your siblings fought with each other—and still do—most of the time you were visiting your parent. Then all of a sudden it was time to go, and nobody had a good time.

One solution to this problem is to have separate visits for each of you. The hard part about that is that you must wait a longer time between visits. The good part is that you and your parent have each other all to yourselves for one whole visit. When just the two of you have the chance to spend time together, you can get to know each other better. You can really talk about things. You may find that the two of you are actually spending more time together than you did when your parents were married. As well as being parent and child, the two of you have the chance to become friends.

Grandparents and Other Relatives

You and your parents weren't the only people affected by the divorce. Other relatives felt it too.

Sometimes grandparents and aunts and uncles take sides. Your mother's relatives may have taken her side, and your father's relatives may have taken his—though it doesn't always work that way. Sometimes Dad's relatives side against him, or Mom's relatives side against her. You felt that you couldn't take sides, even if your parents tried to get you to. You belonged on both sides, but those other relatives might not have been so reluctant to say "She's right! He's wrong!"

If some relatives took sides against the parent you lived with, maybe those relatives stopped seeing you or stopped calling or writing. To be loyal to their side, they felt they couldn't have any contact with you. Or maybe if they did continue to see you, they were always saying bad things about one parent.

How can grandparents and other relatives take sides like that and turn their backs on you or try to convince you that one parent is no good? It isn't fair, of course. They were unhappy about the divorce, too. They didn't like to see their children, or their brother or sister, suffer. They didn't like seeing your family split apart. But, like you, they were helpless to do anything, even though they had very strong opinions about who was right and who was wrong. One way of showing their disapproval was by taking sides, even when that meant ignoring you. So you may have lost touch with relatives who meant much to you, and that's another hurt for you to bear.

Since those other relatives aren't as close to the situation as you and your parents are, they may have gotten over their bad feelings more easily and sooner. If you haven't done it already, you might try calling them or writing them a short note—just to say hello. That may be all that's needed for things to start up again between you and them. There's no guarantee they'll be ready to begin again, but it's worth a try. Not all relatives stay away because they're taking sides. Some are just plain confused. They don't know what to do, how to act. They don't know whether you want to see them anymore. They might be very pleased to hear from you and have the chance to see you again.

Some grandparents, aunts, and uncles, become closer during and after divorce. They want to help everybody however they can. If your relatives did that, you may have found that when you needed someone to talk to, they were the best people of all. They listened, they understood better than your parents did, they cared.

Parents Dating

After a while one or both of your parents began dating other people. However long they waited after the divorce, it was probably too soon for you. It's usually true that parents get over a divorce before their kids do, and there they were going out on dates, going to parties, having fun, while you were still feeling miserable. It was really upsetting. You had this dream that your parents would get back together again, that you'd all be a happy family again. How could that happen if they dated other people?

Besides, it was embarrassing. They were acting silly, getting all dressed up, asking you if they looked okay, worrying about making a good impression. They weren't acting naturally. They weren't acting like parents. They were acting like teenagers.

They wanted you to make a good impression, too—to be polite and act interested and carry on conversations with their dates, to like the people they went out with—and the dates probably tried to make a good impression on you. Maybe they asked you all sorts of dumb questions about school and what you liked to do. Maybe they brought you presents all the time. As far as you were concerned, they were acting phony. They weren't really being nice. They were just trying to prove to your parent how wonderful they were and trying to bribe you into liking them.

But you weren't going to let anybody take the place of either of your parents. You already had a mother and a father, and they belonged together. This dating could lead to marriage, and you didn't want that to happen.

Maybe some of the people your parents dated were okay. They didn't act phony. They didn't try to bribe you. They didn't ask you how old you were and what grade you were in and what books you were reading and whether you liked ice cream every time they saw you. They could actually be fun to be with. You might actually have liked them—if you weren't careful—and that confused you. "If I like my mother's boyfriend, am I being disloyal to my father?" "If I have a good time with my father's girlfriend, will it hurt my mother's feelings?" Sometimes it was hard to know what your real feelings were. Did you dislike your parents' dates because they were unpleasant people, or just because your parents were interested in them? You really didn't want your parents to marry other people, and if you were too friendly, maybe they would. How could you be friendly with someone you liked and still let everybody know you were loyal to that other parent? It was safest to be cold and indifferent. Even if you liked some of those people your parents dated, it was best for you if they'd go away. You wanted to make sure your parents knew you weren't going to let any stranger take Mom's or Dad's place.

Of course, that kind of behavior might have caused a lot of trouble between you and one or the other of your parents. You didn't think it was fair that your parents could mess up your life by getting divorced and then looking for new mates. Your parents didn't think it was fair that you could interfere in their lives by being rude to the people they liked.

Not all kids are upset or angry when their parents begin to date. Some are glad to have other adults as part of their lives. They don't necessarily feel that liking a new person is being disloyal to Mom or Dad. They understand that adding one adult to the people you care for doesn't mean that you have to subtract another adult. Besides, they are glad to see their parents happy again and having a good time.

But whether you approved of anyone your parents dated or opposed all their dates, at some point things began to get serious. You could tell it was happening. One of those people was around more and more all the time, and you all did things together. Then it was time for a "serious talk." Maybe your mother and her boyfriend took you out to a fancy dinner, or your father and you and his girlfriend were all just sitting around the house watching TV. Your parent said, "I have some wonderful news. Chris and I have decided to get married. We love each other very much, and we love you very much, too. We want to make a real home for our family. . . ."

You only heard half the words because your thoughts were making so much noise. Maybe you felt dizzy and sick to your stomach. The last time you had a serious talk like this it was about divorce. This one was about remarriage. The subjects were different, but each time you felt the same.

CHAPTER FOUR

Now You're a Stepchild

In the dream it's all perfect. The day is bright and warm. The whole family is there. Everybody is hugging and laughing. You look wonderful in your brand new clothes, and you feel just as wonderful as you look. You're happier than you've ever been before. At the end of the service the bride and groom kiss, then come over to where you're standing and hug and kiss you. Together you greet every-

one with tears of joy running down your cheeks. Your mother and father have married each other again.

But that's not the way it happened. There was a wedding, yes, but standing where your mother or father should have been, there was someone else. Your dream is torn and crumpled, like the discarded wrapping from a wedding gift.

So Now You're a Stepchild

So now you're a stepchild, member of a stepfamily. If both your parents have remarried, you're actually a member of three families. That first family will always be your family, though your parents divorced. It's a very real family in your mind, even though it's a kind of ghost family in fact. Then there's the family with your father's new wife, and the family with your mother's new husband. If your parents' new spouses have children, they're a part of one or both of your stepfamilies, too. Then there are new grandparents, uncles and aunts, cousins—so many new people in your life you can get dizzy just trying to figure out who everybody is and who is related to whom.

Just as you felt "weird" being part of a divorced family, you may feel that way being part of a stepfamily. Or you may have visions of Hansel and Gretel, prancing around your brain. But you could just as well have visions of Abraham Lincoln—he was a stepchild too. There have always been stepchildren and stepparents. In the past parents usually remarried when their spouses died. The new spouse became stepmother or stepfather to the children.

Today most stepfamilies in the United States exist because of divorce. There are more than 25 million adults in this country who are stepparents, and more than 15 million kids under 19 who are stepchildren. So however strange you feel being a stepchild, remember that there are millions of kids like you living in stepfamily situations. Many of them have experiences, thoughts, and feelings similar to yours.

What Is a Family?

Many stepchildren say that they don't think of their stepfamily as a "real" family. Their idea of a real family is what is called the nuclear family: mother, father, and kids, all living together. It's true that many people think of the nuclear family as the real family, but it's also true that the nuclear family is only one kind of family. Throughout history and in different parts of the world, we find many different kinds of families.

Other Kinds of Families

In "extended" families three, and sometimes even four, generations of people live together—grandparents, parents, children, sometimes great-grandparents, and maybe some uncles, aunts, and cousins. Children grow up and

marry and have children of their own. Grandparents die.
But the family stays put and continues. In many places
outside the United States, the extended family is the normal family. In the United States the extended family began
to fade away as people left the countryside and their
farms to work at jobs in the cities. The extended family
works well for farming. There are more people to work
the land. They all work together in the same place. The
land belongs to all of them. It's natural that they all live
together. But when family members leave their homes to
go to many different jobs, it's hard to hold everybody
together in one place.

Some societies, past and present, are polygamous.
That means one person can have several spouses. Most
polygamous societies allow men to take several wives.
Some allow wives to take several husbands. All the
spouses and all the children make up a family. In some

cases children refer to all their father's wives as Mother, or all their mother's husbands as Father.

Tribes and clans are larger groups of people that are much like families. Though not everybody is related by birth, members of tribes and clans have very strong bonds with each other—much stronger bonds than they have with people outside the tribe or clan.

What all kinds of families have in common is that "bond." A bond is a very strong connection. The bond may be called love or loyalty. It may be based on blood relationship; or shared experiences, ideas, beliefs, and values; or mutual support and protection. In the nuclear family all those things are part of that bond. Explaining the family bond, the poet Robert Frost wrote: "Home is where, when you have to go there, they have to take you in."

One of the reasons that your stepfamily may not feel like a real family to you is that you don't share a bond with your new stepparent. From the instant you are born you have that bond with your parents, and as you live and grow together, the bond gets stronger and stronger. When a new adult steps in to stand where one of your parents stood, you don't automatically have a bond with him or her. That doesn't mean you can't ever have it or won't ever have it. But it takes a long time for a bond to develop, and without that bond the stepfamily doesn't seem like a real family.

There's no one kind of right or real family. Stepfamilies are real families—families of a different sort, just as extended families, polygamous families, tribes, and clans are families of a different sort. All kinds of families have certain things in common, such as keeping a home, rearing children, sharing experiences. But also, each kind of family has its own special problems and possibilities.

What Is a Stepparent?

Is a stepparent really your parent? Legally, no. Legal parents are the mother and father who gave birth to the child, or adoptive parents who have gone to court and signed legal papers to adopt children that aren't their own biological offspring. A stepparent may be legally married to one of your parents, but that doesn't make him or her legally your parent.

But just because a stepparent isn't legally a parent doesn't mean he or she won't try to act like a parent. Many kids get angry when their stepparents make rules and tell them what to do. "You're not my real parent," they say. "You can't boss me around!" Kids feel this way for different reasons.

If you feel angry, maybe you think that your stepparent is trying to replace your other parent. So you hang onto that parent as tightly as you can in a funny kind of way—by resisting your stepparent. You just want to make sure everybody knows where you stand.

It could also be that you're still hurting very much from the divorce. It takes a long time to get over such deep wounds. While you're still mourning the breakup of a marriage and the loss of a parent, another person steps in and a whole new life is supposed to begin. You're not ready for it. It makes you angry to think you're expected just to forget about what's happened and go along as if everything is just dandy. It's not dandy for you, and you don't want anybody to forget it.

Even if you're happy to have a stepparent, you may feel a little confused about what a stepparent is supposed to do and how a stepchild is supposed to act. For that reason it's a good idea from the very beginning for stepfamilies to talk about what everybody's wondering and expecting. It's hard for you, as a kid, to start these kinds of family discussions, particularly if you're feeling bad. Perhaps you could bring up the subject first with your parent. "I don't really understand what a stepparent is supposed to be." "Do I have to do whatever he says?" "Do I have to love her?"

The adults make most of the rules for the kids, and enforce discipline. A stepparent is one of the adults in the family. By marrying your parent, your stepparent was agreeing to share these responsibilities, along with the other responsibilities of keeping a home and providing for a family. But being told what to do and being disciplined by a stepparent are sometimes hard to take. Nobody, you think, but your parents has the right to discipline you. But what about teachers and principals, even some baby-sitters? What about grandparents? The fact is, there may be a whole bunch of adults who tell you what to do. Mostly you just take it for granted. But when it's a stepparent, you don't always take it for granted. You rebel, you resist, you fight it. You're not going to let anybody else take your parent's place. You'll never feel about anybody else the way you feel about that parent. If they expect you to accept this new person as your parent, they'd better think again.

Both stepchildren and stepparents often think they're expected to love each other. Here's a piece of news for you: *You don't have to love your stepparent.* You may not want to love your stepmother because it would make you feel disloyal to your mother. You may have decided not to love your stepfather so he won't get the idea that he can ever take the place of your father. Even if you *like* your stepparent, you may not *love* him or her. You certainly can't be expected to love a stepparent right away with the same strong, deep love you feel for your parents. We'll discuss this subject more in chapter five.

Stepping . . .

When you stepped into the new family, you added a bunch of new words to your life—stepfamily, stepparent, stepfather, stepmother, stepchild, stepbrother, stepsister, stepgrandparents, stepcousins, and on and on. Who knows, maybe you even got a stepdog and a stepcat.

All the "step" words come from the Old English word *steop*, which means "bereaved." Bereavement is the sadness of loss. You are bereaved when you lose someone important to you. In Old English a *steopbearn*—a stepchild—was a bereaved child, an orphan, a child whose parents had died. We add the "step" onto family words to explain the special kinds of relationships that happen when parents remarry.

All those "steps" sound like hiccups. They are unpleasant and clumsy on the tongue and in the brain. Many stepchildren and stepparents feel uncomfortable saying them. They would like a more graceful way of explaining their relationships to each other. "Father's new wife," "Mother's new husband," "Father's wife's children," "Mother's husband's parents," "Father's wife's brother's children," of course, are even clumsier, and some of those terms take a computer to figure out.

It would be nice to find simple words that explain the new relationships without making them seem so odd, so tacked-on. (Some people use words such as "mixed" family or "blended" family, which have a more pleasing sound. That's okay for the family, but it wouldn't work with other words—"blended child" sounds as if it's a kid who's been made into a milkshake.)

Maybe we won't find the right words until people begin to feel that stepfamilies themselves are not odd, but just different kinds of families with different kinds of problems and challenges.

CHAPTER FIVE

Stepfamily Problems

Some magazines show pictures of dream houses. The houses are like works of art. Every room is perfect. There are large picture windows with views of gorgeous gardens and terraced lawns, or stained glass windows or skylights. There are beautiful oriental rugs and polished furniture. There are spotless fireplaces or indoor barbecues or sunken livingrooms. There are wood-paneled libraries or

studies. There are oil paintings or tapestries hanging on the walls. There are swimming pools or tennis courts or brick patios or wooden decks. And very often there are no people in the pictures.

People get the floors dirty. People bang up furniture and break dishes and spill milk on the rugs and leave dirty clothes lying around. Lawns turn brown. Weeds grow in the garden.

Nobody lives a dream life in a dream house. When one or both of your parents remarried, they hoped, after all the troubles, for a dream-house life. They hoped the new family would be a perfect dream family, and maybe you did too. But you all found that it didn't work that way. Almost overnight troubles appeared—scratches on the furniture, stains on the carpet. And the dream house soon looked like any other house where people live.

When you started having problems, maybe you thought it was because you were in a stepfamily, not a "real" family with both parents. You forgot all the troubles your parents had when they were married. You thought, once again, "If my parents were together, we wouldn't be having these problems. Everything would be perfect." But any family without troubles is a TV family, a cartoon family, not a real one. Stepfamilies have special problems, true. But all families have troubles of one kind or another because they are families—individual people with different personalities, different needs, different desires, different opinions, all living together. The only way to be absolutely sure everybody gets along is for everybody to live alone in a cave. (And don't pick a cave with a bear in it!)

So just because your stepfamily has problems, it doesn't mean there's anything seriously wrong with it. The best thing to do when problems arise is to try to figure out what they are and what to do about them.

Not Enough Attention to Go Around

One problem you might have is one that started before your parent remarried. Your parent started paying attention to this other person and stopped paying attention to you. Even after the marriage he or she continued to act like a teenager, all silly and romantic, and forgot you were alive. You felt jealous.

Jealousy is hard to admit. You don't want to seem spoiled or greedy for attention. It's hard to admit jealousy, but it's easy to feel it. You like affection and attention from the people you love. When you're feeling good and strong and sure of yourself, you don't need constant attention and reminders of love. You know that the people you care about care about you, too, even when they're not right there showing you or telling you that they do. But when you're not so sure of yourself, when you're feeling shaky and worrying about whether those people care for you, you need more from them. Divorce and remarriage can make a kid feel shaky for a long time. You begin to wonder if you're really loved. You need lots of attention. And here's this new person, this new husband or wife, getting all your parent's attention. Does anybody care about you anymore?

Because it is so difficult to admit your need for more attention, maybe you don't. Maybe you just feel more and more sad and lonely. You act unhappy and don't talk to your parent or your stepparent except when you can't avoid it. You think, "If they don't care about me, I don't care about them!" Or maybe you do things that get you into trouble—arguing all the time with them or with your siblings or stepsiblings, ignoring chores, not doing your schoolwork. Getting into trouble gets you all sorts of attention even if it isn't exactly the kind you'd like.

By not talking about what you're feeling, things keep getting worse. Every day your unhappiness grows. Is there any way you could ask for what you need? You needn't have a tantrum and shout, "I need attention!" But maybe you could say, "Mom, would it be okay if you and I went somewhere, just the two of us?" or "Dad, could you and I go to a movie together?" That should be a pretty comfortable way of reminding your parent that you need some time alone with him or her.

Wicked Stepparents

There are all kinds of stories about wicked stepparents. Everybody knows how nasty Hansel and Gretel's stepmother was. In some old myths stepparents are the murderers of the parents they replace.

Kids may feel particularly angry and resentful of a stepparent who was involved with Mom or Dad before the marriage ended. They may blame that stepparent for the divorce and hate him or her for being the cause of all the misery that followed. It's good for kids who feel that way to come to understand that the other person didn't cause the divorce. Marriages that break up end because partners are unhappy with each other and see no chance of things getting better. That is a problem between husbands and wives; no new person can cause that problem.

But whether they blame their stepparents for the divorce or not, many kids complain that their stepparents are mean—maybe not so bad as the evil ones in the old stories, but plenty mean even so.

It could be that your stepparent is stricter than either of your parents. Your stepparent may expect you to behave in ways you've not been expected to behave before. If so, that's very difficult to get used to. It's particularly hard to get used to all sorts of new rules and regulations after you've had some independence. You got to be more independent when you were living with one parent. You were expected to do a lot of work, to take a lot of responsibility, to do many things for yourself. You felt like a partner in the single-parent household, not just a kid to be bossed around. Then your parent remarried, and your stepparent doesn't treat you like a partner. You're told what to do too much; you're punished too often; you don't feel trusted. The remarriage took your independence away.

You know enough about parents (and teachers too) to understand that being strict isn't necessarily the same thing as being mean. Meanness is just to cause hurt. It's calling names or teasing cruelly or shouting or beating or other kinds of bad treatment. It's big punishments for little mistakes. Strictness may mean many rules, many chores, early bedtimes, discipline, and punishment for breaking rules. Strictness may be hard to take, but it can be fair. Meanness is never fair.

When you're feeling upset about the way your stepparent is treating you, it isn't so easy for you to tell the difference between strictness and meanness. Think about it carefully. If your stepparent is beating you, or locking you in your room or in a closet, or is yelling at you all the time and tormenting you and calling you names; if you are left alone most of the time, or you don't get enough to eat, you must tell someone who can help—your parent, a grandparent, a teacher or counselor at school. No adult—not a stepparent, not even a parent—has the right to be cruel to a kid.

If you decide your stepparent isn't really being cruel but is still too strict for you, you should talk about that, too. Maybe you can start by talking with your parent. "I don't think it's fair that I have all these rules all of a sudden. She's treating me like a two-year-old." It's best if you and your parent and your stepparent can all discuss it together. It may make you nervous to think about such a discussion. Plan everything you want to say very carefully before you speak. You might begin by saying it's hard for you to get used to behaving in a brand new way. "We didn't used to have to think about table manners. Now, all of a sudden, we have to remember to keep our elbows off the table and use our napkins and say 'excuse me.' It's hard to change so fast. In our old family, table manners weren't so important. In this family they are. It's confusing." "Mother always helped me clean my room. Now you expect me to clean the whole house without any help at all, and when I don't, you get mad. I'm not used to that."

You may find, if you're able to talk about it, that your stepparent will make some changes and become less strict. Or maybe there won't be any change. Maybe *you'll* have to change, by getting used to a strict stepparent. If you can't seem to do anything to change the situation, find somebody who will understand what a tough time you're having. One 11-year-old stepchild got together with three other stepchildren in her school and started an Anti-Stepparents Club. What they do is complain to each other about how bossy their stepparents are. They say it helps just to talk to somebody else who understands.

Confusion About Love

By the time you became a stepchild you'd seen plenty of pain. Your own suffering over the breakup of your family was hard to bear. Just as difficult for you was watching your parents suffer through the divorce. Your pain and

theirs continued as you all learned to adjust to the strange new lives you led with somebody missing. Kids who have gone through a divorce are very sensitive to even the smallest things that can cause hurt. You may worry that any relationship you have with your stepparent will cause somebody pain, and you may not know what to do.

What if you really care for your stepparent? What if you really feel you could love him or her? Will that hurt the parent who isn't there? And what if you don't love your stepparent? Maybe he or she seems to love you, but you don't have the same feelings. Will that hurt your stepparent? Or will it hurt your mother and father if you don't love their new mates? You're stuck. If you feel any way at all, it seems that you can hurt somebody. So you figure it's safest to try not to feel anything or to hide your true feelings.

It is important for you to understand that loving one person doesn't mean taking love away from someone else. Throughout our lives we continue to meet new people and make new friends. Some of these people we love, but we don't stop loving people we have loved before just because we start loving someone else. If you marry some-day and have a family, you will love your husband or wife and your children. That doesn't mean you'll stop lov-ing your parents or your dear friends. Love doesn't work that way. If you love your stepparent, your other parent should understand there's no limit to the amount of love you have. (That doesn't mean that parent might not be a little jealous—just as you have felt jealous when someone else got attention and affection you'd have liked all to yourself. If you feel your parent might be a bit jealous of your stepparent, take care to show that parent a lot of love.)

On the other hand, maybe you don't love your step-parent. Your mother wants you to love your stepfather so you can all be a happy family. But you don't. Your father wants you to feel your stepmother is just another mother. But she's not your mother, and you don't love her. Your mother wants you to love your stepfather because *she* loves him. Your father wants you to love your stepmother because *he* loves her. But you can't be expected to love a stepparent just because a parent does.

For one thing, you may be a little nervous about loving a stepparent, about getting too attached. You've been hurt once by a divorce. What if you get close to your stepparent and there's another divorce? You're going to take your time and be very careful before you care too much about anybody again.

For another thing, love hardly ever happens right away. It takes time to develop. As people get to know each other better, as they share what's important to each of them, work through problems, give comfort and support, they may begin to love each other. Your stepparent is a brand new person in your life. You haven't had the time to get to love each other. Don't feel guilty about that. Don't blame yourself and think you are a bad person.

Finally, you may never love your stepparent. There's nothing wrong if you don't. Your stepmother is somebody your father chose to be with. You didn't choose her. Your stepfather is somebody your mother chose to be with. You didn't choose him. They got married. You didn't. Even if you'd like to feel for your stepparent what you feel for your parents, you may never do so. Maybe the most you'll ever be is just friends.

It's good if both you and your stepparent can be relaxed about this business of loving each other. When you try to love someone you don't, or act as if you love someone you don't, everything becomes tense and unreal. You may be extremely polite and force yourself to smile and laugh all the time. But you're not being yourself, and you're putting a lot of pressure on yourself to act a part you don't feel. That can make you miserable. You can only act that way for so long before all your emotions come spilling out, and there may be a terrible fight with all sorts of shouting and crying. Everybody's so surprised. Where did all those angry feelings come from? With all the other problems stepfamilies can have, trying to love a stepparent when you don't is one problem you can do without.

If you're worried that your parent will be hurt if you don't love his or her new spouse, it will help if you can explain what you're thinking and feeling. "I know you want me to love my stepfather. I wish I could say that I love him. But he's not my dad and I don't know him very well yet. I don't feel about him the way I do about you and Dad. Maybe I will someday. I don't know." If you aren't comfortable saying that kind of thing to your parent, then maybe you'll just have to keep saying it to yourself. If someone is hurt by your not loving your stepparent, you are not responsible for the hurt.

Conflicts Between the Two Families

In a boxing match the fighting stops when the bell rings. As you found out, divorce isn't a bell that stops the fighting between your parents. Their battles may have continued long after the divorce, and even when there are not more fights, bad feelings can remain. If your mother still complains about your father and gets angry at him, her new husband—your stepfather—may take her side and complain and be angry, too. If your father still thinks your mother is irresponsible and still makes sarcastic remarks about her, his new wife—your stepmother—may take his side and make the same kinds of remarks.

It was hard enough for you to deal with the conflicts between your parents when it was just the two of them slugging it out. You felt stuck in the middle, not wanting to hear the fights, not wanting to hear all the complaints and criticism and accusations, not wanting to take sides because you loved them both. Now it may be that you're stuck between three or four adults who never seem to miss the opportunity to say or do hurtful things. "Your father's late again. That's just like him. You can never depend on him. I'm certainly glad your stepfather's not like that." "Your father gives your mother all that money for you kids and she won't even buy you a new pair of sneakers? What does she do with it, buy new clothes for herself? Your father told me how selfish she was." And once again you feel you're being pressured to take sides against a parent you love.

The anger and bitterness parents feel toward each

other, even after they marry other people, shouldn't involve you. Can you tell them it hurts you to hear them say mean things about each other? Can you ask them not to do it when you're around? Can you tell them you feel pressured into taking sides and you don't want to take sides?

Making Comparisons

It's normal for kids to compare their stepfathers with their fathers and their stepmothers with their mothers. The trouble is, those comparisons can get all tangled up in emotions.

What if your stepmother is an excellent athlete? She plays in tennis tournaments and swims and cycles, and wants to share those interests with you. Because your mother is not very good at sports, you'd feel disloyal to

her if you enjoyed participating in them with your step-mother. So even if you'd like to learn tennis, you refuse your stepmother's invitations so that you won't be dis-loyal to your mother.

Think about all your friends. Aren't there some who draw better than others, or run faster, or are smarter? Still, they are all your friends—the clumsy artist, the slow runner, the average student. You don't like or love people because of their abilities, but because of who they are. Admiring stepparents and what they do doesn't mean lov-ing parents less.

Often the comparisons work the other way around. Maybe you think that everything your parent does is absolutely wonderful and your stepparent is just dull and ordinary. Compared to your stepparent, your parent is Superman or Wonder Woman. "Mom is a terrific skier and takes me skiing all the time. My stepmother can't even play hopscotch." "Dad is an expert on food and always takes me to fantastic restaurants. My stepfather only likes junk food." By making these comparisons, you are being very loyal to your parent. But you aren't giving your stepparent much of a chance, and maybe you don't want to give your stepparent a chance. You think it's your mother and father who belong together, but that's obvi-ously not what your mother and father want. They've chosen new partners with whom they think they can be happier than they were with each other. They're not mak-ing the same kinds of comparisons you are.

Even if you think your stepmother and stepfather are real duds, it might help you to try to understand why your parents chose them. You might try to appreciate a stepparent for the same reasons your parent does. Maybe your stepmother's not a great athlete, but she's very patient and is a good listener. Maybe your stepfather doesn't know anything about gourmet food, but he is thoughtful and fair and never loses his temper.

Making comparisons between parents and stepparents makes *you* miserable. You either feel guilty about being disloyal or you feel cheated out of a "superparent." Accepting both parents and stepparents for just who they are can make getting along much easier for you.

Stepsisters and Stepbrothers

Cinderella had it bad. Not only did her stepmother make her do all the work and sleep in a pile of rags, but also she had two stepsisters who bossed her around and didn't do anything themselves.

When your parent remarried, you may have gotten stepsisters and stepbrothers along with a stepparent. That could have made everything even more difficult for you. If you were an only child before, all of a sudden you weren't. If you were the oldest child before, maybe you found yourself with older stepsiblings telling you what to do. It's hard enough to get used to a stepparent. Getting used to new brothers and sisters, and to being in a new position in a new family, can seem almost impossible.

There are more kids needing the adults' attention. All of a sudden you don't have the long talks you used to have with your mother. Those other kids are always there. All of a sudden you and your father don't go to the movies alone. Those other kids always come along. Maybe you gained some brothers and sisters, but you feel as if you've lost a parent. Not much of a trade.

And what about fairness? Does your stepfather treat his kids better than he treats you? Do you have more chores? Do you get scolded more often? Are there rules that they're used to but that are brand new to you? Does your stepmother do fun things with her own children and leave you out? Do your stepsiblings' grandparents send them presents and not send you any? Or take them on trips and not take you? Do they have family jokes and family stories that you don't understand? Do they make you feel that you just don't belong? Do you feel as if you are a stranger in this new family?

Putting two families together to make one new family is very difficult indeed. Each family has its own rules, its own way of doing things. One family may have strict discipline. The other family may be relaxed about discipline. In one family the adults may make all the decisions. The other family may have meetings to decide important issues. One family may vacation in the mountains, and the other may always go to the seashore. In one family the kids may choose which chores they do; in the other the adults always tell kids which chores to do.

In your first family, with your parents, you had a long time to get to know each other. You knew each other's ways of doing things, each other's moods, each other's likes and dislikes. You learned how to talk with each other, how to joke and tease. You developed rules often without knowing they were rules. In the stepfamily you start again from zero.

Unfortunately, not all families recognize the importance of discussing all these differences and problems. It's pretty hard for you to say, "Okay, we're going to have a meeting to work out our problem." Or, "Okay, get in the car. We're going to a counselor." So what can you do?

You have to talk to somebody about what's bothering you. You can't keep it all inside. That will just make you feel worse, more angry, more alone. Can you have a private conversation with your parent? Think about the best way to bring it up. It probably won't work to say, "He's not fair. He's always mad at me. His kids are spoiled. I hate them all!" That may simply upset your parent and make him or her feel like defending your stepparent instead of listening to you. Instead, you could say, "I need to talk to you. I'm really confused about what the rules are and what I'm supposed to do. I feel as if I'm always getting into trouble and that I can't do anything right." Or, "I feel left out when she does things with her kids and when they tell family stories that I don't know anything about." By speaking that way, you're talking about your feelings without attacking anybody else. That will make it much easier for your parent to listen to you. Then maybe your parent can tell your stepparent, and you all can begin working on the problems. What's important is to say what you're feeling without blaming anybody. When you start blaming, people get ready for an argument.

If you feel shy about talking even to your parent about these problems, you might try talking with your stepsisters and stepbrothers about them. After all, they're stepchildren too. Maybe they're feeling that everything is unfair. Maybe they're feeling left out. You may find that you and your stepsiblings can help each other understand the adults better. You may find it's easier to approach the adults if there's more than one of you. And, if nothing else, you may find that you have somebody else to complain to when you're fed up.

Adoption

William Shakespeare wrote, "A rose by any other name would smell as sweet." But Sally Jones thinks the name Sally Fish stinks. She won't change her name even though after the marriage her mother and stepfather are Mr. and Mrs. Fish.

Names in stepfamilies can be a real problem. Some kids feel uncomfortable having last names that are different from a parent's and a stepparent's. For one thing, you have to do a lot of explaining when classmates and teach-

ers ask, "Why is your name different from your parents'?" "Well, you see, he's not my father. He's my stepfather, and my mother changed her last name to his when they got married. But I kept my own. . . ." You can get pretty tired of saying that over and over again. You don't much like talking about the divorce and the remarriage and the fact that you're a stepchild. The name business just keeps bringing those subjects up. It would be so much more convenient if you all had the same last name.

On the other hand, many kids are happy to keep their father's last name. They're proud of it. It's their name, too. They wouldn't change it for anything.

Often the issue of last names is connected to the subject of adoption. Because they wish to make stronger the bonds that hold the new family together, some stepparents wish to adopt their stepchildren. Stepparents are not related to their stepchildren. Marriage is a legal relationship between your parent and stepparent. No such connection exists between you and your stepparent. Adoption makes a legal connection. By law your stepfather becomes your father (and you change your last name), or your stepmother becomes your mother—with all the responsibilities to care for you that a parent has. If your stepfather adopts you, your father no longer has those responsibilities. It's the same for your mother if your stepmother adopts you.

Your stepparent's wish to adopt you is a way of saying, "You are important to me, so important that I want to be a true parent to you." It's nice to have someone care that much about you. Maybe it would make you very happy to be adopted by your stepparent. It would certainly show you that your stepparent didn't think of you merely as part of the package that came along with the marriage. It could give you a real sense of belonging in the new family.

But maybe you don't want to be adopted. You already have a father, and you don't want to exchange him for your stepfather. You already have a mother, and you don't want your stepmother to take her place.

If the subject of adoption comes up in your stepfamily, you must let everyone know exactly what you want. You may worry that you'll hurt your stepmother's feelings if you say you don't want to be adopted. You may worry that you'll hurt your father's feelings if you say you'd like to be adopted by your stepfather. (In almost all cases you can't be adopted unless your parents give their permission.) But *your feelings are most important of all.* When a parent or stepparent asks you what you feel about being adopted, answer honestly. If it's hard for you to speak about these things, write a letter. (See page 106 for an example.) Don't let such an important decision be made without you.

"Where Do I Belong?"

The ancient Chinese poet Tu Fu once wrote that he felt "lost between heaven and earth." All people want a home, a place where they belong. You have two families—two parents, one or two stepparents, perhaps brothers and sis-

ters and stepbrothers and stepsisters. You live in two
houses. Is each of them a home, a place where you
belong? Do you belong in one place and not in the other?
Or do you feel you don't belong anywhere at all?

Different rules.   It is so hard to have two families.
Each family has its own way of doing things, and these
ways may be very different. At one house you're allowed
to stay up as late as you want. At the other you have a
very definite bedtime. At one house you have to clean
your plate. At the other, nobody cares whether or not
you eat your vegetables. At one house kids and adults
play together. At the other house kids must play quietly
by themselves and not disturb the adults. You can certainly add other differences to this list. Those differences
are very hard on you. You spend time at your father's
house getting used to living in a certain way. Then you go
to your mother's house and you must do things in an
entirely different way. Like travelers who suffer from jet
lag by flying across many time zones, you suffer from
family lag, moving back and forth between two different
worlds. So it may always seem to you like "Mom's house"
and "Dad's house," but never "my house."

It would be wonderful if you could get everybody
together—parents, stepparents, siblings, stepsiblings—to
work out the differences that are so tough to get used to.
Imagine yourself a judge dressed in black robes, banging
your gavel. "Order in the court! Will the Smith family
and the Jones family please rise. Smiths and Joneses, you
are driving me crazy with your different rules and differ-

ent habits and different ways of doing things. In the name of fairness and justice I hereby decree that from now on there shall be only one set of rules for both families. Chores shall be the same at both houses. Standards of behavior shall be the same. Bedtimes shall be the same. Rules about using the phone and watching television shall be the same. If you fail to agree on one set of rules, I'll throw you in jail until you do agree!"

A nice fantasy, that one. But it isn't likely that the two families in your life will ever sit down to agree on a single set of rules. Just as much as individual people are different from each other, so are families different from each other and must function with the rules and standards that seem to work best for them.

So, what can you do about "family lag?" Try to let each family know how hard it is for you to live by two sets of rules and to remember which rules apply at which place. "At Mom's place I only have to clean my room once in a while, but here I get into trouble if I don't clean it every day." "At Dad's house I can joke and tease with Dad and my stepmother. Here if I do that, you say I'm being sassy and you send me to my room." You hope, when the two families begin to realize how hard it is on you, commuting between two lives, that they'll try to make some changes.

Betwixt and between. Or maybe you have another problem. You feel just fine in both places. You get along with your stepparents. Both families are equally strict or lenient. You have your own room at each house.

You don't have any trouble feeling that you belong. Instead, your emotions constantly pull you from one place to another. When you are at home in your mother's house, you think often and sadly about your father, and wish to be with him. When you are at home in your father's house, you miss your mother and want to be with her. The minute your body goes to one place, your mind goes to the other place. Even though you feel you belong in each place, you can never seem to get your whole self together. You can never seem to enjoy fully being with your father because you miss your mother, and vice versa. For you two homes, even two *good* homes, are not better than one. You want to have everybody you care about—that may include stepfamilies as well—under one roof. That way you could relax and enjoy being "at home."

There's no perfect solution to this problem of having your emotions pull you in two directions. It happens because you care so much. And you can't stop caring. The best thing to do is to talk about the feelings when they appear. Don't let emotional pressure build up until you become sick with worry and confusion. Tell someone how you're feeling—maybe a parent or other relative who you know will understand, or another stepchild who might be feeling the same way.

Holidays, birthdays, vacations. Holidays, birthdays, and vacations can be another real problem when you have two families. With whom do you spend Thanksgiving? At which house do you celebrate your birthday? Do you have to go visit your father during summer vacation when you'd rather be at home swimming and bike-riding with your friends?

Kids worry very much about being fair to both parents, about not hurting their parents' feelings when it comes to holidays, birthdays, and vacations. Maybe you spend every spring vacation with your father and stepmother. Maybe this year you want to spend it with your mother and stepfather who would like to take you on a trip to Mexico, but how do you tell your father? Won't he be hurt? Maybe you've always spent the entire summer with your mother and your stepfather. This year you'd like to spend some time there, but you'd also like to spend some time at home near all your friends. If you tell that to your mother, will she think you don't love her?

Do you sometimes have a hard time talking to someone—particularly an adult—about something that's really important? Do you get nervous and confused and forget to say all the things you wanted to say? Maybe you could write a letter instead.

Dear Mom,

How are you? How is Arthur? I'm doing very well. I got an A on my last math test. Boy was I surprised! Last week on the way to school I left the back gate open and Stony got out. The dog catcher got her and we had to pay $25 to get her back. Was Dad every mad!

It's only two more months until summer vacation. I'm really excited about seeing you and

Arthur. Are we going to drive to Grandma Kate's again? I hope so.

Something's kind of bothering me about vacation, Mom. I miss you so much during the year. Sometimes I get so lonely for you I cry myself to sleep. And I'm always really excited to come and stay with you. But the trouble is, all my friends are around here. And when I spend the whole summer with you, I don't have any chance to be with them. Even though I know a couple of kids where you live, it's not the same as being with my friends here.

I was wondering if it would be okay with you if I spent half the summer with you instead of the whole summer. Please don't think this is because I don't want to be with you. I do. It's just that it's hard to be away from my neighborhood and my friends for a whole summer. It's almost as if I have to start all over again making friends with my old friends every fall.

I heard this man on television says it's not the *quantity* of time parents and kids spend together, it's the *quality* that's important. Will you write to me soon and tell me if it's okay with you if I spend half the summer with you and half the summer here? I love you very, very much, and I miss you!

Hugs and kisses,
Jeanette

Dear Dad,

I just got back from Dr. Bundy's office. She says I can get the cast off my arm next week. Then I can write you letters with my right hand again! Mom says before I start roller stating again I'll have to get wrist guards. She doesn't want any more broken bones. Neither do I!

I miss you a lot. I wish you lived closer so we could see each other more often.

I have something to ask you, and it's kind of hard for me. Mom and Sam are going to Mexico during spring vacation and they said I could go along if I wanted to. But Mom also said she knew how important my visits with you are and she doesn't want to interfere with them. The trouble is, I want to do both things. I never get to see you enough. And I haven't ever had a vacation with Mom and Sam. Do you think you and I could see each other some other time than during spring vacation? Maybe we could have an extra two weeks this summer and go camping then. Would that mess up your plans? Mom says it's okay with her to do it that way. If that won't work, then I'll come for spring vacation. I don't want to lose our time together.

I'll write you next week after I get my cast off. I love you and miss you very much.

Love,
Toby

It's Not All Just Problems

Even though it may seem that way sometimes, it isn't just problems that make a family or a stepfamily. A family is people caring for each other, helping each other, learning from each other, enjoying each other, sharing with each other, growing together. With all its special problems, a stepfamily can have special pleasures.

You can learn new things from everybody you meet. A stepparent is a new person in your life, a person who can introduce you to new interests and experiences. Maybe your stepparent is very different from your parents. Maybe your stepparent is a pilot, or a scuba diver, or a stamp collector, or a musician, or an artist, or a sailor, or a gourmet cook, or a mechanic, or a computer programmer. From him or her you can learn about things you couldn't from either of your parents. What a good opportunity to expand your world, having another adult willing to share interests with you.

Your life in a family is like the ripples on the surface of a lake when a stone is tossed into the water. The little waves make ever-larger circles as they move away from the center. Your life makes ever-larger circles as you have new experiences, develop new abilities, grow more independent, relate to new people. Learning to relate to new adults other than your parents is part of the necessary business of growing up. Every year in school you must relate to new teachers. Outside school there are other adults who are part of your world—coaches, music teachers, doctors, dentists, and more. With each of them you develop a unique relationship, not like the relationship you have with your parents. It can be the same with stepparents. Developing a relationship with a stepparent, different from all the other relationships you have, can be an important growing experience. You can think of him or her as another one of those people who have become a part of your growing up. Probably none of those people will be as important to you as your parents are. Your parents are the ones who started you on your way in this world. Your stepparent, though, can help you continue.

The Two Families Together

One big wish many stepchildren have is that the two families will someday be comfortable together. At birthday parties both families will be there, with all the grandparents, and everybody will get along just fine. Parents won't be mad at each other. Stepparents won't be jealous of previous spouses. Siblings and stepsiblings will play happily together.

It's not very realistic to hope for more than just an occasional pleasant get-together on a holiday or birthday. It's not very realistic to hope that somehow, magically, your two families will become just one big, happy family—your family. If your two families can get together once in a while without lots of tension and bad feelings, then once in a while you'll be able to enjoy being with all the people you care about at the same time.

CHAPTER SIX

How Does A
Stepparent Feel?

Many people dream of getting married and having a family. They don't dream of doing it all at once. Yet that's just what happened when your parent remarried—your stepparent got an instant family. Just as there are problems being a stepchild, there are problems being a stepparent. In fact, your stepparent may have some of the *same* troubled feelings about the new family that you do.

Time and Attention

While it may seem to you that your stepparent has taken your parent away, your stepparent may feel that he or she must compete with you for your parent's attention. Especially when they're newly married, couples want to spend as much time together as possible. Newlyweds with no children have plenty of time to continue to get to know each other and to enjoy their romance. Newlyweds with a ready-made family often feel that they left romance at the front door. Just as you want time alone with your father, so does your stepmother. Just as you want to go to a movie or take a long walk with your mother, so does your stepfather. Just as you feel jealous of all the attention your stepparent seems to be getting, so may your stepparent be jealous of you. Stepparents often complain, "I thought I was marrying one person. It turned out I really married several." "I thought after we got married we'd continue to go to cozy little restaurants and have romantic evenings alone together. We haven't really been alone together since the wedding. The most romantic thing we've done is hold hands in the supermarket while the kids were two aisles away getting some breakfast cereal."

New stepparents with children of their own aren't so much bothered by having children around beginning the very first day of their marriage. They're used to it, though even they may be a bit jealous of the attention their new mates give the children. But a new stepparent who has never had children will probably be surprised to discover

how much attention goes to the children—surprised and
jealous.

Nobody likes to admit feeling jealous. It seems so
selfish. Yet jealousy is a very real and natural feeling. It
will help your stepparent understand you better to realize
that you may be feeling jealous, and it will help you
understand your stepparent better to realize that he or she
may be feeling the same way.

Being an Outsider

When two people have a baby together, they learn about
parenting as the baby grows. Over the years the parents
and the growing children learn more and more about each
other. They get to know each other's likes and dislikes,
each other's strengths and weaknesses. They develop special ways of communicating, sometimes just with looks
and gestures instead of words. They have pet names for
each other and family jokes that nobody else understands.
They remember the Thanksgiving when Grandpa dropped
his glasses into the sweet potatoes and the vacation when
the car broke down. All these shared experiences and
memories are part of the family bond.

A new adult steps into the family—a stepparent—
who doesn't share this bond. The stepparent feels like an
outsider. If you've ever moved into a new neighborhood
and changed schools, you know what that feels like. You
are nervous and shy. You watch everybody very carefully,

looking for some place to fit in. You want very much not be to the new kid. You want very much to belong. It may be hard for you to imagine that an adult can feel that way, too. But very often that's exactly how a new stepparent feels, even if he or she doesn't show it.

Instant Parent

Besides wanting to belong, your stepparent wants to be a good parent for you. That doesn't mean that your stepmother wants to replace your mother or that your stepfather wants to replace your father. Stepparents should realize that they can't replace parents. But they want to help take care of their stepchildren, help guide them and teach them, help them grow.

As you've seen, parenting is something that people learn about gradually, usually making a lot of mistakes as they go. Your stepparent may want to be a perfect parent right away, even though he or she hasn't been with you over the years to learn about parenting and to learn about you. Most parents know they can never be perfect parents. They know they will continue to make mistakes, and they also know they can learn from those mistakes. If they feel strong and confident, they can forgive themselves their errors, and they know their children will forgive and forget, too. But new stepparents often don't feel strong and confident. They feel pressure to prove themselves right away so they will be accepted into the new family. So when they make mistakes or seem to fail, when they get angry or fight with their stepchildren, when they scold too much or discipline too harshly, when they misunderstand what their stepchildren do or say, they feel hurt and terribly guilty. The more guilty they feel, the harder they try to be perfect, and the harder they try to be perfect, the larger their little failures seem to be. They get tense and bad-tempered. They worry that their stepchildren hate them. They worry that their new mate will think that the marriage was a mistake.

It isn't only stepparents who want perfection. Often a parent feels so guilty about the breakup of the original family that he or she is determined to make this new family a perfect one. That parent may often expect perfection from a new spouse. That kind of expectation makes the pressure a stepparent feels even greater.

It's best if your stepmother realizes that she can't be a perfect parent. It's best if your stepfather understands that he must get to know you gradually, the way your parents did. It's best if everybody—you, your parents, your stepparent—realizes that a stepparent can't become an instant parent any more than you can become an instant son or daughter.

If you can all relax about this and give each other plenty of time, a good relationship can develop. You shouldn't expect the best or the worst. Be patient. Forgive each other mistakes. Find ways to let each other know you're trying.

Instant Love

Everybody knows that parents are supposed to love their children. When parents don't seem to love a child, we judge them harshly. Stepparents aren't the same as parents, yet most of them think they are supposed to love their stepchildren. When they don't, they judge themselves harshly.

Earlier you read that there's no rule that says you have to love your stepparent. Neither is there a rule that says your stepparent must love you. But it's difficult for stepparents to believe that. "How can I love my husband and not love his daughter?" "How can I love my wife so very much and not feel the same way about her son?" But why not ask another question: "How can two people who don't know each other very well be expected to love each other?" The problem is what stepparents may expect of themselves.

The love between parents and their child begins even before the child is born. It begins as the baby grows in her mother's body. Love grows as the baby grows, as parents dream and plan their family life. They choose a name for the child. They buy a cradle and blankets and toys. They make a spare bedroom into a nursery. They imagine what the baby will look like. Then they experience the birth of the baby and feel great wonder and joy that together they have made a new life. They see that the baby has her mother's eyes, her father's nose. The baby is part of them. They feed the baby and bathe her. They stay up all night when she is sick. They teach the infant to walk and to talk. They watch the toddler's body and personality develop. They worry when the child rides her bike around the block for the first time. They feel proud when a teacher says she is an excellent student. They wonder whether they are good parents.

All of these emotions and shared experiences are involved in the love parents and children feel for each other. Your stepparent has shared none of this with you. How can he or she be expected to love you the minute he or she walks in the door?

Stepparents say one of the hardest things for them is to admit that they don't love their stepchildren. They're afraid they are "bad" if they don't feel that love. They're afraid they'll hurt their new mates or damage their step-children if they don't feel that love. So instead they try to hide their feelings. They keep a guilty secret. Their guilt makes them terribly unhappy and makes it harder for them to have a comfortable relationship with you.

Just as you need to know it, stepparents need to know that it's okay not to love their stepchildren right away, or ever. Some of the best step-relationships are built on friendship and respect. You can give that to each other without feeling guilty that there is not love also.

Conflict Between the Children

Stepparents who bring their own children into the new family feel very bad when their children and stepchildren don't get along. It's not unusual for kids to take out all their unhappy feelings—anger, hurt, jealousy—on their stepsiblings. They may tease their stepbrothers all the time, or say nasty things to their stepsisters, or not talk to the stepsiblings at all. One boy took all his little stepsister's stuffed animals into the basement and cut them into pieces with a pair of scissors.

When stepparents see their own children being hurt, they naturally get very upset. They may take their own children's side against their new spouse's children. They may get very angry at their stepchildren, which makes the stepchildren more angry so they treat their stepsiblings even worse. If you fight with your stepbrothers and stepsisters, it makes it much harder for you and your stepparent to get along. Your stepparent may get mad at you a lot. You may feel he or she is picking on you, being mean and unfair. Your stepparent may feel *you're* being mean and unfair, picking on your stepsiblings. The only way out of this vicious circle is for you both to figure out what

you're really feeling and talk about it. If you're truly angry with your stepsiblings, then it's best to get the reasons for that anger out in the open and try to solve the problem. If you're mad at everything—at the divorce and the remarriage and the enormous changes in your life— you certainly shouldn't take that anger out on your stepsiblings.

Not Enough Time Together

Some stepparents, who really want to get to know their stepchildren better, complain that there's never enough time. "I'd love to spend more time with her, go to ball games and movies, take hikes, go biking. But every weekend and every vacation she goes to her father's house."

These stepparents feel frustrated, and probably a little bit jealous of those other parents their stepchildren spend so much free time with. "He's here all week, and I'm telling him to do his homework and clean his room. Then on Friday night he goes off to his mother's, and they have a marvelous time playing all weekend. I don't like being the police officer. I wouldn't mind so much disciplining and enforcing rules if we could also spend some time having fun together. I must seem like the 'wicked stepmother' to him."

This kind of situation isn't something you should feel bad about. It's a problem built into nearly all stepfamilies. When you have two families, there's never enough time for both of them. It isn't your responsibility to miss visits with your parent so you can be with your stepparent. But being aware that your stepparent may be frustrated about not having enough time with you can help you better understand how awkward it can feel being a stepparent. And it can make you feel pretty good to know that your stepparent might not be overjoyed about "getting rid of you" at every opportunity.

CHAPTER SEVEN

Helping Yourself

"Only the dreamer can change the dream," wrote the poet John Logan. Perhaps even long after your parents' divorce and remarriage to new mates, you've held onto a dream that your mother and father would get back together again and you'd all live happily ever after. It's a lovely dream. And it makes you miserable. It makes you

miserable because you want so badly for it to happen, and it doesn't happen. It almost never happens that divorced people remarry each other.

Why not change your dream? Why not dream of two wonderful families—your mother and stepfather, your father and stepmother, and you and your brothers and sisters and stepbrothers and stepsisters? Why not change your dream and work to make it come true? There are any number of things you can do on your own to work on your problems and make family life happier for yourself and everybody else.

Identify and Express Your Emotions

The biggest problems that most stepfamilies have are emotional ones. If stepfamily members have good and positive feelings about each other, then most disagreements dissolve quickly. If stepfamily members have strong negative feelings about each other, then even the tiniest difference can seem like an unclimbable mountain.

It's important for you to say what you're feeling. Negative feelings get stronger and stronger the longer you keep them inside. But before you can express your feelings honestly, you must know exactly what they are. Saying "I hate my stepfather!" isn't enough. Hidden underneath that "hate" are other feelings. Are you jealous that your stepfather gets so much of your mother's attention? Are you worried that your stepfather is trying to replace your father? Do you feel guilty that you don't love your stepfather? Are you angry because your stepfather is so strict, or because he treats you almost like a baby, or because when your mother married him, you had to leave your old neighborhood and school and friends and move into his house? Think hard about what you're really feeling. Be very honest with yourself.

Good listeners.   Of course, when your brain is bubbling over with emotions, it isn't always easy to tell exactly what those emotions are. Talking helps. To whom can you talk? Maybe there's someone outside the family who could be a good and helpful listener. Do you have any friends who are stepchildren? They may be having many of the same feelings you are having. Try talking with them, listening to them about what they're feeling. You may learn a lot. If nothing else, it will give you a good chance to get some things off your chest.

If there are no other kids you can talk to, are there any adults? You want to find someone you know won't preach to you or take sides. What about a teacher you really like or a school counselor? Maybe one of your grandparents is very understanding and would be a good listener. If you want your conversations to be private, be sure to say so. What you say should be kept between you and the person you talk to.

A diary. You may not want to talk to anybody right now. If not, try writing what you feel. Get a diary with a lock on it and write everything you're thinking and feeling in there. Every few days read over what you've written. Maybe you can go to some private place and read your diary aloud to yourself. Even if you're not saying the words to anybody else, just saying them can help.

Pen pals. Lots of kids have pen pals. Why not try to find a stepchild pen pal? You might be able to help each other understand stepfamily problems better and give each other some good advice. Find some children's magazines that have ads for pen pals in back and send in your own ad.

> **Wanted:** Pen pal 10-12 years old who is a stepchild. I'm a girl 11 years old who likes swimming, country music, horses, and Dungeons and Dragons. I'm also a stepchild and would like to hear from other kids about stepfamily problems.

Figure Out What Others Are Feeling

Identifying and expressing your feelings are important
parts of solving problems. But there's more to it than that.
It will also help you to try to understand what other people in your stepfamily are feeling. One way to find out, of
course, is to talk with them about the problems. But if the
negative feelings are very strong, it isn't easy to start right
out by having a serious conversation with a parent or a
stepparent or stepsiblings. Instead, you could start by
reading some books on the subject, as you're doing now.
There are other books listed at the back of this one that
deal with the problems of divorce and the problems of
stepfamilies. You might read some of those. You might
even give this book, or other books, to other members of
your family and ask that they read them. Sharing a book
might be a good way to bring up subjects that are difficult
for you to discuss.

      Another way to understand what another person is
feeling is to have an imaginary conversation with that person. Go to someplace private. Sit down and face that person (who isn't really there) and tell him or her everything
that's on your mind. Don't just think it; say it aloud.
When you're finished, pretend to be that person, and
answer yourself. You must try to be very honest when
you speak for that other person. Try to imagine exactly
what it is that person must be feeling. When you're finished being the other person, speak for yourself again.
Keep the conversation going for as long as you want. You
may be surprised to find that you begin to understand

what that other person feels and what you feel. You can have this kind of imaginary conversation once or a hundred times.

Be Your Own Advisor

Here's another imaginary game that can help you deal with stepfamily problems. You've probably read the advice columns in the newspapers. People write to Dear Abby or Ann Landers or somebody else, explaining a problem and asking for advice about solving the problem. You can write yourself a Dear Abby letter, then answer your own letter. Often it's easier to understand problems when you're not so close to them. It's like looking at some paintings. When you stand too close, you can't tell what they are. You must stand back some distance to see them clearly. Writing yourself a letter and answering that letter is a way of stepping back from your problem to see it more clearly.

> Dear Expert,
>
> I am an 11-year-old boy with a big problem. My mother and father are divorced. My mother just got married again to a man with two daughters. My problem is my stepfather. He's not strict with his daughters, but he's very strict with me. When they don't clean their rooms, nothing happens. But when I don't clean my room, my stepfather yells at me. It's not fair. What can I do?
>
> Stepped-on

Dear Stepped-on,

Maybe your stepfather is worried that you
won't mind him or respect him unless he is very
strict. It will probably take some time for you two
to get to know each other before he can relax and
start treating you the way he treats his daughters.
In the meantime your whole family should agree
on some rules for doing chores, and some discipline
when the chores don't get done. Maybe you could
agree to clean your room every Saturday morning.
If you don't, you don't get to play with your
friends until you do. If your mother and stepfather
agree on the rules, then nobody needs to yell at
you. You can also suggest that the rules should be
the same for you and your stepsisters, so everything is fair.

Expert

Write a Letter to Your Stepparent

So many of the problems in stepfamilies happen because
stepchildren and stepparents just can't seem to get along.
Back on pages 83 and 85 you saw how writing a letter to
a parent was one way to discuss things that are important
but hard to speak about. If a conversation with your stepparent seems too difficult at first, you might try writing all
your thoughts and feelings in a letter. That way you can
say whatever you need to say without interruption. You
should be very careful to write only what you're feeling,
without blaming anybody for anything. And, of course,

you won't always communicate with your stepparent by letter. But a letter may be a good way to start.

Dear Dave,

    I'm writing you a letter because it's easier for me to get all my feelings down on paper than it is to say them.

    I know you want very much for me to call you Dad. Mom says you are very happy to have a family and that you think of me as your son. She says maybe someday you'd adopt me.

    I'm glad you married Mom because now she seems so happy. I want us all to be happy. But I can't call you Dad, because I already have a dad. I could never think of anybody else as my dad, even if he died. It isn't that I don't like you. I do. I like the things we do together. I never knew anything about canoeing until you taught me. But I love my dad very much, and I always want him to be my dad. When you introduce me as your son, it makes me feel as if I'm cheating my real dad.

    I hope this doesn't hurt your feelings. I feel very lucky to have you as a stepfather. I wish there were some other word besides stepfather. But I want to keep the word Dad for my dad. And even though it's confusing sometimes that you and I have different last names, I want to keep my dad's last name.

                            Bill

You may even write a letter such as this one and then decide not to give it to your stepparent. Just writing it can help you understand your own feelings better, whether you let your stepparent read it or not. When you understand your own feelings well, then maybe it will be easier for you to bring up subjects difficult to talk about.

Stepfamily Discussions

When people are having problems with each other, it's best if they can talk with each other about them. Does your stepfamily have meetings or discussions to talk about problems? If not, maybe you could suggest that everybody get together to talk things out. If the adults haven't brought up the subject of family discussions, you may feel nervous bringing it up. You might feel most comfortable suggesting it first to your parent. Or, if you have siblings or stepsiblings, you kids could talk about it first, then all go together to the adults with the suggestion.

These family discussions can be tricky. There are usually plenty of strong feelings. People get angry. They interrupt each other. They may argue and shout. They may never get to say what's really on their minds or to hear what's on other's minds.

Family discussions should have rules. Each person should have the right to speak without being interrupted. Each person should listen very carefully to what others are saying. People should not blame or call names. They should say only what they are thinking and feeling, not what they imagine others to be thinking and feeling.

If your family can't have helpful discussions on its own, you might try to find a family counselor. Many people resist going to counselors because they think it means they're weak or even sick. But it isn't weakness to have problems. Everybody has problems. Going to a counselor doesn't mean you need somebody else to solve your problems. Counselors can help families see what the problems are and offer suggestions about solving them. But only the families themselves can make the necessary choices and changes that will actually solve the problems.

Once again, it's not easy for kids to say, "Let's go to a counselor." Do you have a grandparent or an uncle or aunt you can ask to help you bring up the subject? Perhaps you could discuss family counseling with your grandfather, and your grandfather could suggest it to your mother. If not a relative, what about a school counselor?

Another thing that can help a stepfamily more easily discuss its problems is meeting with other stepfamilies. All over the country there are stepfamily associations that help stepfamilies get together and talk about their problems. You might ask a school counselor if he or she has any information about stepfamily groups in your area. Otherwise, you can write to the Stepfamily Association of America at the address listed on page 111 and ask for the address of a stepfamily group near you. When you get the information, give it to your parent or stepparent.

Try to Be Positive and Patient

Sometimes it can seem that a stepfamily is nothing but problems, problems, problems. It can make things easier for you to pay some attention to what's good about your stepfamily. Your father may be relaxed and happy for the first time in a long time. Your stepmother may be interested in many things that are brand new to you—photography or skiing or wood carving—and may share those interests with you. Maybe you get new grandparents and aunts and uncles and they all send you birthday presents. Maybe you got a new stepbrother whom you really like. Appreciating the good things won't make the problems go away, but it can make the problems seem more bearable.

And finally, try to be patient. The stepfamily is a new family. People need time to get to know each other. No family just happens. No family ever stops growing and changing, because the people in it don't stop growing and changing. If you are patient about the growth and change in your stepfamily, you will probably find that many of today's huge problems will just disappear the way a bad dream does when you wake up in the morning.

RESOURCES

For information about stepfamily groups in your area write:
Stepfamily Association of America
900 Welch Road, Suite 400
Palo Alto, California 94304

Books for Kids

Bates, Betty. *Bugs in Your Ears.* New York: Pocket Books, 1977.

Blume, Judy. *It's Not the End of the World.* New York: Bantam, 1971.

Gardner, Richard A. *The Boys' and Girls' Book About Divorce.* New York: Bantam, 1971.

Jackson, Michael and Jessica Jackson. *Your Father's Not Coming Home Anymore.* New York: Richard Marek, 1981.

LeShan, Eda. *What's Going to Happen to Me?* New York: Four Winds Press, 1978.

Mann, Peggy. *My Dad Lives in a Downtown Hotel.* New York: Avon, 1974.

Neufeld, John. *Sunday Father.* New York: New American Library, 1976.

Platt, Kin. *Chloris and the Creeps.* New York: Dell, 1973.

Platt, Kin. *Chloris and the Weirdos.* New York: Bantam, 1980.

Robson, Bonnie. *My Parents Are Divorced, Too.* New York: Everett House, 1979.

Rofes, Eric, ed. *The Kids' Book of Divorce.* Lexington, Mass.: Lewis Publishing Company, 1981.

Sinberg, Janet. *Divorce Is a Grown Up Problem.* New York: Avon, 1978.

Sobol, Harriet Langsam. *My Other-Mother, My Other-Father.* New York: Macmillan, 1979.

Stenson, Janet Sinberg. *Now I have a Stepparent and It's Kind of Confusing.* New York: Avon, 1979.

Books for Adults

Capaldi, Fredrick and Barbara McRae. *Stepfamilies.* New York: Franklin Watts, 1979.

Galpher, Miriam. *Joint Custody and Co-Parenting.* Philadelphia: Running Press, 1980.

Gardner, Richard A. *The Parents' Book About Divorce.* New York: Bantam, 1979.

Grollman, Earl A., ed. *Explaining Divorce to Children.* Boston: Beacon, 1969.

Kalter, Suzy. *Instant Parent.* New York: Berkley, 1980.

Maddox, Brenda. *The Half-Parent.* New York. New American Library, 1975.

Ricci, Isolina. *Mon's House, Dad's House.* New York: Macmillan, 1980.

Roosevelt, Ruth and Jeanette Lofas. *Living in Step.* New York: McGraw-Hill, 1976.

Rowlands, Peter. *Saturday Parent.* New York: Continuum, 1980.

Salk, Lee. *What Every Child Would Like Parents to Know About Divorce.* New York: Werner, 1978.

Spann, Owen and Nancy Spann. *Your Child? I Thought It Was My Child.* New York: Pocket Books, 1980.

Troyer, Warner. *Divorced Kids.* New York: Harcourt Brace Jovanovich, 1979.

Turow, Rita. *Daddy Doesn't Live Here Anymore.* Garden City, N.Y.: Doubleday, 1977.

Visher, Emily B. and John S. Visher. *Stepfamilies: Myths and Realities.* Seacaucus, N.J.: Citadel, 1979.
Wallerstein, Judith S. and Joan Berlin Kelly. *Surviving the Breakup.* New York: Basic Books, 1981.

Index

About the Author

Buff Bradley has written several books for adults. His first book for children was the acclaimed *Endings* (Addison-Wesley). He has also written a documentary film script and two books of poetry.

Buff Bradley is married and lives in Palo Alto, California. He has three children, two of whom were his stepchildren before he adopted them.